CHRIS RACKLIFFE

It's Good to See Me Again

HOW TO FIND YOUR WAY WHEN YOU FEEL LOST

IT'S GOOD TO SEE ME AGAIN:
HOW TO FIND YOUR WAY WHEN YOU FEEL LOST.
ISBN: 9798648967069
Copyright © 2020 by Chris Rackliffe. All rights reserved.

Thank you for purchasing an authorized edition of this book and for complying with copyright laws by not reproducing, scanning, or distributing any part of it in any form without prior permission.

BOOK DESIGN BY JACQUI JADE O'DONNELL
Typography: Gotham, Machiato, Times New Roman

To all my heartbreaks:
Thank you for giving birth to me.

Contents

PART 1
Lost 9

PART 2
Resisting 39

PART 3
Accepting 77

PART 4
Choosing 117

PART 5
Embracing 153

PART 6
Found 184

1
Lost

CRACKED OPEN

Ever since I can remember, people have called me some version of the nickname *Crack*. I've been called *C-Rack*, *Crack Attack*, *Crackle*, and *Crack Life*. I've pretty much heard it all.

That's what I get for being named Christopher Robert Rackliffe.

Once someone realized that my first initial and last name basically spelled *Crack Life*, there was no going back. At first it really annoyed me. I wanted nothing to do with the nickname *Crack*. I'd cringe a little bit each time a classmate of mine would say, "Hey *Crack Life!*" But as anyone with a name that lends itself to something catchy will tell you, there's not much you can do.

After making peace with my fate, I decided to accept my nickname, make it into my persona, and beat everyone to the punch in the process. Now *Crack Life* is my full-on digital identity. All of my social media profiles are @crackliffe and my resume has never had my full name on it—only my nickname. I can't tell you how many people have "cracked up" over the years while hearing me spell out my Instagram handle or email address. "Who is this *Crack Life* character?" People ask. The whole thing makes me feel like I pulled a MacGyver or Olivia Pope—strategizing my way out of an uncomfortable situation I disliked but could not change. The only choice I had was to accept it. So I did.

This has become my approach to life: Accept what I can't change and choose to change everything else. I wasn't always this way. I found out the hard way that our lives are defined by our relationship with Change. When something happened I didn't foresee or expect, I did everything possible to avoid or deny it. I ran away. I numbed. I didn't want to feel the pain or fear or uncertainty. I wanted to feel safe. I wanted to feel in control. I wanted things to be predictable.

But that's not how life works. Life is inherently unpredictable. Things are constantly changing. As humans, it's natural to get scared, go into fight-or-flight mode, and resist what Change has to teach us. But this reflex also stifles and disorients us. We feel like we can't shape our reality when we try to change the unchangeable.

Thankfully, life doesn't have to be this way. You don't have to live in a permanent state of resistance. I discovered firsthand that there's another way. We can choose to accept the ups and downs of life. We can choose to accept Change. We can choose to release what's not in our control and focus on what is.

Accepting Change is one of the healthiest things you can do. It's healthy to give up resisting and accept reality. It's healthy to stop playing the victim and accept healing. It's healthy to accept that not everything is under our control. This is how you clear your mind and free your spirit so you can find your way forward. Whenever you find yourself struggling with Change, ask this question: *Do I have the power to change this, or must I accept it instead?*

And yet, not everyone chooses to accept what they can't change.

For some, it seems like Change is chipping away at you, little by little, until you feel like you no longer recognize yourself or your life. You ask: *Why can't things be the way I imagined? Why do I keep getting blindsided by Change?*

I'll tell you why. You have a God-given right to choose. When you use that right to defy what you can't change, you choose against yourself. You waste your time. You focus on all the wrong things. You avoid what you are meant to learn. You become disoriented. That is why you feel so lost.

Change is the Universe's way of cracking open our hearts so something new and unexpected can burst forth despite all of our efforts to resist. It is a wake-up call. It shows up as the death of a loved one or the loss of your job. It happens when you go through a breakup or you lose everything you own in a fire or a flood or a tornado. It rears its head when you get a diagnosis you never saw coming. It happens to everyone eventually and no one is immune.

The Japanese art form of kintsugi illustrates this phenomenon. It is said to have started in the late 15th century when a damaged tea bowl was sent to China for repair. Instead of gluing or stapling the pieces back together, which were both common solutions for the time, they were rejoined with powdered gold, illuminating the same cracks they were meant to conceal. What was once a common tea bowl became transformed into an elevated piece of art—something far more valuable because of its wear and its repair. The cracks became the seams for it to shine.

Kintsugi shows us that what we feel breaks us, makes us. What doesn't kill us doesn't just make us stronger; it makes us more intricate, more distinguished, and more exquisite than before.

When we get knocked down in life, it can be easy to feel that we are broken, destroyed, or irreparable—that we should be discarded. What kintsugi shows us, though, is that when we surrender ourselves to be restored, we aren't just repaired; we are reborn. We aren't just pieced back together; we become brighter, bolder, and more beautiful than we ever imagined we could be.

Each time Change shows up in your life, you get to choose whether to accept or resist. Too often we choose the latter. We get scared. We build our walls ever taller. We deny what Change can teach us. We avoid being cracked open. Try as you may, you can't outrun reality; you can't resist what can't be changed. The walls must fall.

Don't be afraid. When your walls come crashing down, you'll discover something beautiful: A cracked heart isn't a wounded heart; it's a whole heart revealing itself. That death or diagnosis or divorce turns into the catalyst for positive growth because it reminds you that life is precious. All you have is right now. All you can do is accept what can't be changed and choose to change the rest.

> A cracked heart isn't a wounded heart;
> it's a whole heart revealing itself.

This is not just *your* truth—it's *the* truth. You are here to grow and learn—to ride the tides of Change. Even if you feel like you lose your way for a time, you can never truly be lost. You will always find your way back to yourself if you remember you have the power to choose to accept Change or create it.

Things will happen to you in life that you never saw coming. Your heart will get broken open again and again and again. The promise of this book is to help you transform your relationship with Change, to show you how to stand confidently in your power to choose. Change is a natural part of what it means to be human. Even when we make all the right choices, we will encounter Change. It is impossible to outrun. Remember this: When a situation arises that you never saw coming, you still have a choice. You can always choose how you relate to it. You can always choose how you show up. You can always choose to embrace Change. This book will show you how.

My nickname may be *Crack Life*, but we're all living a cracked life. Because Change continually cracks us open. I'm here to tell you to let it. Or create it. Either way it's how we expose our gold.

THE LAW OF LIFE

The sun shines through the living room windows, painting my kitchen a fresh shade of morning gold. The rays fade as the sun hides behind a cloud. A car drives by and another car takes its place. Birds chirp cheerfully in a nearby tree. A voice from the street beckons another voice and a conversation is born. The sun returns, illuminating the white walls in canary yellow. I walk to the window and face the light, allowing it to coat my face before the sun fades away. The world is waking and setting itself into motion once again.

There's something magical about the morning. There's a sense of potential, a feeling of freedom, a state of surrender as we shake our slumber and are greeted by the sun once again. Night gives way to day. Darkness intermingles with light. Stillness is stirred.

There's a certain reverence about the changing of the guard that occurs at dawn. It's a moment that so many discard as monotonous and mundane, but deep down it reveals a truth as old as time. *Everything changes*, my intuition senses. *Nothing gold can stay.*

President John F. Kennedy reflected on the inevitability of Change and the constant motion of our existence: "For time and the world do not stand still. Change is the law of life. And those who look only to the past or the present are certain to miss the future."

We don't have to search far and wide in our lives to see the evidence of this truth. Your five senses are proof that Change is constantly unfolding. Pay close attention and you will find that everything you sense is just a relative difference—a change from what came before it. You hear sounds that weren't there before. You see movement as a perceived shift in position relative to you. If nothing changed, nothing could be perceived. Life as we know it would cease to exist because there would be nothing left to experience. Change is the very definition of what it means to live because life is experienced only through Change.

Change is the natural order of things. One moment turns into another turns into another. Energies shift and then shift again. Nothing ever stays the same except for Change itself. So what happens when we resist, defy, or avoid Change? We try to make a moment something other than what it is. We interrupt the natural order and create disorder in our lives because we're attempting to defy a fundamental law, like trying to make rain fall upward. It's simply impossible. The laws of our universe won't allow it. The very fabric of our reality is imbued with Change. When we defy it, we defy ourselves. We lose our way. This process unfolds simply and predictably over time:

- Change appears in the form of something unforeseen.
- We feel uncertain, anxious, frustrated, worried, and fearful at this unexpected turn of events.
- We resist Change by creating stories of how we think things should've turned out.
- Our stories cause us to suffer because they are incongruent with reality.
- Suffering is disorienting and makes us give up our power of free will.
- When we feel powerless to choose, we abandon ourselves and feel lost.

There's no telling what we'll do when we feel lost. We spiral. We waste precious time. We fall out of alignment with ourselves. We block our blessings. We make unclear choices. We subvert our best interests. We act out in fear. We numb. We refuse to feel our feelings. We bury our love with resentment. We reach for any coping mechanism possible. We fall from grace.

These are all attempts to protect us from pain. They are also the birth of suffering. And that is something far worse because we choose it for ourselves. Even when it's the last thing we want.

THE FIRST ARROW

It was the most intense physical pain I've ever felt. The only thing that I could muster between sobs and swords of shooting pain were screams of, "Why me?"

My soccer teammate and goalie, Zac, charged from behind me as we defended against an offender, the three of us colliding mid-air. As gravity pulled us back down to earth, Zac and the striker both landed directly on my leg. Seeing the severity of my expression, Zac carefully crawled off the pile-up on the floor of the indoor arena.

I knew something wasn't right before I could lift my head to see it for myself. I pulled my torso up just enough to evaluate the situation. As my eyes met my leg, I let out a blood-curdling scream.

"Why me?"

My ankle and leg were broken and my body was in a state of shock. The fluorescent lights felt blinding as adults and teammates alike crowded around me in disbelief. Suddenly the room started spinning. My dad gently rested my head on the floor using his hand as a pillow, beckoning to another parent to call 9-1-1.

My shrieks went on for minutes as I bemoaned my fate until eventually they were replaced by the wailing of an approaching ambulance. An eerie silence swept over the arena while tears streamed down each side of my face and onto the floor below.

My father, who was also the coach of my team, ran to collect his coat from the sidelines as the paramedics arrived, giving a knowing nod to the assistant coach to take over in his absence. The stretcher below me was a cushion of comfort as I was whisked through the hallway and out of the building. In the ambulance my dad cupped my hands in both of his to keep them warm, reassuring me that it was all going to be okay. Everything felt slowed down and sped up at the same time.

THE SECOND ARROW

I felt like a complete and total failure.

During another indoor soccer game growing up, I made a last-ditch effort to block a shot from the other team's striker. But instead of deflecting it, I ended up accidentally scoring a goal on my own team. In the final seconds. Of the championship game.

I couldn't even look at my teammates on the way out of the arena after the match.

My dad tried to comfort me in the car on the way home. "I know you're down on yourself right now, Son, but several parents came up to me after the game to tell me how impressed they were with how hard you played. You prevented a lot more goals tonight than you allowed. Remember that," he said.

His kind words were cast upon a distorted mind—one that was intent on believing I had messed it all up. I was young and soccer felt like my entire world. I couldn't help but feel responsible for the loss. *You cost the team the championship*, I thought. *You let everyone down*. In my heart of hearts, I knew I blew the entire season with that one mistake.

The truth, however, was that a lot of mistakes were made that night. And not just by me. Goals were allowed. Shots were missed. Passes went awry. Players were fouled. My mistake was magnified by the intensity and recency of the moment, but I shared in the culpability of the loss with everyone else on the team. I just refused to see these truths through the thick fog of negative narratives whirling in my head.

There's a Buddhist parable that describes this phenomenon. It characterizes pain and suffering as two arrows. The first arrow represents our physical pain. This process is automatic. When you break a bone, for instance, pain is your body's physiological response to the disturbance in your system. Your body speaks to you through pain. It says, *Ouch that hurts!* If you're smart, you listen and respond. You do what you need to heal and recover.

Mental pain is really no different from physical pain. When pain arises in the mind, it serves the same purpose: It signals a disturbance in the system. The only difference between physical pain and mental pain is that we tend to listen to the former and we tend to ignore the latter. Before the physical disturbance passes through us, we attempt to make sense of it and ascribe meaning. We replay the event over and over in our minds in an attempt to rationalize it. But it cannot be rationalized because pain doesn't operate by our moral standards. It just happens.

When we fail to make sense of our pain, we decide to take matters into our own hands. We choose to make something up instead. We create stories that exaggerate its importance and impact. We ascribe arbitrary importance to the event. We would rather falsely encode the memory with meaning than truthfully admit that it was unpleasant and move on. We make a huge mistake when we think of our pain in this way instead of allowing ourselves to feel it and let it pass. We keep the pain alive by shrouding it in stories about why it happened, how bad an experience it was, and how we didn't deserve it. This is the definition of the second arrow, of what it means to suffer. You choose to keep your pain alive when you keep retelling stories about it.

The first arrow lodged itself in my leg. I listened to the pain and removed it, and eventually healed. The second arrow lodged itself in my heart and stayed there. I unapologetically refused to take it out. And I suffered as a result.

THE GREATEST CONVERSATION

You never know where a broken leg or broken heart will lead you. *Where* it leads isn't really the point. It's *what* you stand to learn, *what* Change can teach you about appreciating your life right now that really matters.

Life is an ongoing conversation with Change. And it favors those who converse in a brave, open, and empowering way. We are all on a journey with no set path. Not everyone learns the same lessons at the same time and in the same way. But your life is always trying to connect with you and show you what you need to learn. Change is one of the ways life aims to teach us. Change is neither good nor bad. It is simply a principle of life.

Make no mistake: It can be scary to greet Change without knowing what awaits you on the other side. The key is to remember that you are being led, to believe that there's a force that guided you here and that the same force will continue to guide you every step of the way. Trusting in this presence is the foundation of what it means to have faith. Having faith means believing in something bigger than ourselves, knowing that things are unfolding for our ultimate benefit, and taking things one step at a time even when we can't see where the road goes. Faith is the choice to surrender our burdens so we do not bear them alone.

It's easy to have this level of trust when we think things are going well because they're unfolding according to our expectations. It's also easy to fall off the wagon when it gets the slightest wobble—when we'd rather trust our own two feet and our own willpower. It's a huge bummer when you want things to stay the way they are but then they unexpectedly shift. It feels much easier to avoid Change than to accept it. It's easy to fall into the trap of distrust and disenchantment that arises when things suddenly shift.

Too often when things don't go according to our plan we rush to the disempowering instead of empowering questions. Too often we abandon our faith when fear creeps in. Too often we question instead of trusting. Life changes in a flash. It can end in a flash, too. Why spend it fighting and resisting things we cannot change? Why ask questions we don't want answered? Why feed our fear instead of our faith? Why would we want to put that energy forth at all? We know there's no going back to the way things were. Yet instead of empowering ourselves to forge forward we feel disempowered and stumble backward. We ask: *Why did this have to happen to me?* Instead we could be asking: *How can I come to see this as a blessing? How can I deepen my faith? How can I accept this and move on?* Those are the questions we truly want the Universe to answer.

What we really want to know are all the ways Change might help us grow, might deepen our trust and faith. Instead, we challenge Change to a boxing match, insisting that we duke it out to prove that we're right. But we lose every time. There's only one way to win, and that's to stop fighting, remove the gloves, and go in for a hug. *Welcome back old friend*, we'll think. *It's good to see you again.*

THE STORIES WE TELL

If you pay close enough attention, you'll notice that you have a story for every painful memory in your life, for every moment of significant Change. You just weren't aware of them. That's because these stories sit below our conscious level of awareness, in a realm we rarely explore. This level is primitive and primordial. It is the most basic part of our brain—of our unconscious or unaware mind—that controls automatic functions necessary for us to stay alive. Breathing is an example of an automatic activity that is controlled by the unconscious mind. We breathe in and out without needing to actively think about it. This part of the mind is active each and every hour of the day to ensure that it continues to happen.

Your stories are also housed here. Stories come in different shapes and sizes, but they all try to accomplish the same goal: Keep us safe from pain at all costs. But they are different from other unconscious functions in a major way. Unlike their instinctive neighbors, our stories limit us from ever really living at all.

A story is a coping mechanism for pain. It is a bundle of beliefs encoded with the energy of the past. This mechanism ensures that whenever it is triggered it will root you right back in that pain. This is the very definition of the second arrow, of mental pain, of suffering. When we suffer, we're taken out of the present moment. We can't focus. We can't show up for ourselves. The pain of the past consumes us once again. It feels fresh, like the aftertaste of a meal you hated that lingers on your tongue. But it is stale. You're experiencing pain that is days, months, or even years old. The past is never laid to rest when a story is in control. These buttons linger beneath the surface just waiting to be pushed and reactivated by any situation or experience.

A story is nothing more than a group of thoughts you've believed in to help protect you and keep you safe, a painting of the past whose brushstrokes are seared into the dark recesses of your mind. These are imprints, not blueprints. They don't tell the actual story of what happened and they don't actually sustain or protect you. Rather, they tell a version of the past that sustains and protects your ego, that keeps you locked in a victim mentality and roots you in fear. Ask yourself: *How would I feel if I gave up telling myself this story?* You'll start to see just how desperately we cling to these narratives, hoping that they will provide us with a respite from pain, only to discover they are the cause of most of it in our lives. Because they won't ever let us put it to rest.

A WEB OF LIES

I couldn't bring myself to break the news.

I was heartbroken for the second time in as many months—and deeply humiliated. "Can you please text them for me? I don't want to talk about it but I want them to know the latest," I messaged my cousin, Haley, enlisting her assistance to inform some of my best friends of the breakup.

"Of course, I'll let them know," she said. "Don't be down on yourself. You'll find someone new in no time and they'll be a better fit for you." But her kindness was shut out by the stories of shame that surrounded me.

"I don't know. I guess so. Love you," I said despondently.

The sticky stories of the past were woven like a spider web in my mind. *You'll never find someone better*, the voice of fear whispered within. *You weren't good enough for him*, it continued. I crawled back under the covers and wept. The pain of past and present met on my pillowcases, merging with my tears. The stories of prior heartbreaks were resurfaced once again. My mind declared a state of emergency and summoned its army of stories from the depths of my unconscious. Mental martial law was in effect.

It's usually pretty easy to spot someone who's caught in a web they've woven, acting on a painful story from their past. There's a frenetic energy about them that shrouds their presence because they've wrapped themselves so tightly with the security blanket of their story that they struggle to see clearly or rationally. They lack conscious awareness of their thoughts and actions. What could be a cocoon has turned into a tomb.

Our stories take hold of us and turn us against ourselves, like a Trojan horse sent to destroy us from within. There are as many stories as there are grains of sand, but there is one culprit that causes way more negative stories than any other factor. It is a product of our fear, an ingrained part of the unconscious. It is our shame.

Shame is fear incarnate. Our shame stories are dangerous because they are hurtful and damaging. They are also incredibly common. Everyone you know has likely experienced a shame story at some point or another. Shame stories take many forms, but sometimes they sound like: *I'm not enough*, *I'm too much*, *I can't do that*, or *I don't deserve that*.

As you and I know from personal experience, whether backed by shame or not, our stories are stubborn, sticky, and strong. Our inner narratives are sharp and cunning. They seep down into the depths of the psyche and latch on, rearing their ugly heads to wreak havoc in our lives at a moment's notice. These powerful pockets of negative energy sit untouched and unresolved in the unconscious part of the brain, waiting to be triggered by an event that reminds you of what it was like when you endured a similar painful experience. The unconscious mind senses *it's happening again just like before*, and the pain of the past rips us out of the present in a manner that can only be described as a type of mental whiplash.

This phenomenon has been called by many names. In Hinduism

and Buddhism, it is referred to as a *samskara*. A samskara is a recollection or imprint of the past that you carry with you. These mental impressions have far-reaching impacts for how the individual interacts with the events of his or her life. Another name for this phenomenon is *schema* or *schemata*. These are simple psychological terms for how we develop frameworks for future understanding. Another phrase that references this same occurrence is *pain-body*. Popularized by spiritual teacher and bestselling author Eckhart Tolle, the pain-body is described as an accumulation of emotional pain from the past that is stored in the energy field of an individual. This same experience is also commonly referred to by other names like negative narratives, limiting beliefs, or stories. I will use these terms interchangeably throughout the book, but I am always referring to a singular phenomenon: Our unconscious inclination to resurface the pain of the past.

This force is powerful, but it is not indestructible. It has a clear and direct weakness: The light of your awareness. Awareness diffuses the power of the pain-body because it takes it from the unconscious realm into the conscious one. Once you summon a story, schema, or samskara into your conscious awareness, you can do something different that you may have never considered before. This choice could even change your entire way of living. It's the choice to let go of the pain and reach for something else, like peace or joy. It's the choice to recognize and replace your story before you act on it. This is the bedrock of what it means to release our suffering. When we make the conscious choice to defy our stories, we signal to the Universe that we are ready to mend.

And then we finally do.

THE POWER OF FREE WILL

At any given time on any given day, you're likely making dozens of different choices. By the time you've gotten dressed and eaten breakfast, you've selected which emails to read, which notifications to check, and which form of caffeine will jolt you into a semi-coherent state for your first meeting. And those are just the choices you make before 10 o'clock.

We make hundreds if not thousands of different choices each and every day. These choices can be quick and straightforward, like the ones we make first thing in the morning. Or they can be conscious and deliberate, like the ones we make when we buy a car or house or decide whom to marry. Choices come in all shapes and sizes but there are really only two categories of choices: Conscious and unconscious. With every choice we make we are consciously or unconsciously choosing to wield our willpower again and again.

The ability to choose is nothing short of incredible. In any given moment, you have the power to consciously create your reality, to breathe life into your dreams. Your life is a sculpture. You get to shape and mold it, removing what no longer makes sense and adding elements that give new dimension and character to your art. This is your masterpiece. You get to choose which form it takes.

These decisions are yours and yours alone to make. That's why it's imperative to treat your choices with careful consideration and conscious awareness. Everything you choose creates your reality. Most of this happens unconsciously and automatically. That is also a choice. You get to choose if you will consciously make your choices or whether you will run through life on unconscious autopilot. Pay attention to the choices you make and you can completely transform your life.

Choices require energy. Conscious choices require more energy than unconscious ones. This is what it means to pay attention. You're providing the energy of your awareness in exchange for information. Not every choice needs to be made consciously. We don't have the time or energy to do that. In fact, it would be impossible to get anything done if we lived life that way. However, if you decide to make more conscious choices than unconscious ones you'll notice your energy start to shift.

When you make conscious choices that support your health, happiness, and highest good, a magical moment occurs: You actually have more energy! When you use the energy of your conscious awareness to invest in yourself, you earn a return on your investment. Your energy multiplies. As a maker of choices, this is what it means to stand in your power. Never underestimate your power to consciously choose. It is a force that's available to you at any time. It is God-given and inherently yours.

Our choices have consequences. Any given choice can have one of two consequences. The first consequence is that our choices bring us closer to the truth of who we are. This is what it means to live in alignment with your spirit. You have a deep reverence for life when you realize that you are fortunate just to live it. Life feels good when we're in this space. Not just on a surface level but deep down in the seat of the soul. We live out our purpose when we choose to make decisions that support our highest good. We unlock joy, ooze happiness, and emanate abundance this way. Things just feel *right*.

The second consequence is that our choices can push us further away from the truth of who we are. This is the essence of what it means to feel lost. We choose to ask disempowering questions. We choose to personalize the pain of the past and make it about us. We choose to invest in our stories and protect our negative narratives.

Life feels suffocating when we've stumbled from the path meant for us. When we make choices that don't support our highest good, we feel like our free will is slipping away, like things are spiraling out of control. Any time you feel lost, it is because you've forgotten your true self and what you're truly here to do. Feeling lost means that you have surrendered your power to consciously instead of unconsciously choose.

At any given time, we are making a number of choices. These choices either support our happiness or detract from it. We take a step closer to fulfillment or we take a step away from it. We take a step closer to honoring the pain of the past by allowing ourselves to feel it, or we take a step away by pushing it back down and denying our feelings. You get to select the route you want to go. No one walks the same path, but we all make the same fundamental choices. *Will I be present today? Can I open my heart once more? Am I able to greet Change with open arms? Can I tolerate pain once again?* The answers to these questions bring us closer to or further from our power. These choices provide a return on our investment or they drain us.

Whenever struggle sets in, whenever you feel lost or like you're slipping away, remember that you can choose again. Reclaim your power to choose and you will never lose your way again. Even when you feel like there is no other choice, you still have the power to choose—even if it's simply to choose to believe that there's another way, or that you're being guided. As long as you are breathing, there is always another choice.

You are the maker of your choices. You have been divinely appointed to exercise your free will as you choose. The key is to make conscious choices. Making a conscious choice simply means making it intentionally. When you make choices with awareness and intention, you reclaim your power, elevate your energy, and create a life that is in line with your values, your purpose, and your spirit. It happens day by day. Little by little, you learn to let go of the impulse to make unconscious choices and let your life run on autopilot. You get tired of reliving the pain of the past, carrying its weight with you from moment to moment. When you arrive at this point in your journey, you know you are ready to choose a different path—one that is more peaceful, more healing, and more empowering. One that is conscious.

Despite all of your best efforts—despite all of the conscious choices you make that feel right at the time—at one point or another you might still feel like you've lost your way. Do not fret or go into fight-or-flight mode when this happens. It's only natural to feel this way. Just remember that you always have the power to make another choice right now. We make better choices based on the information at our disposal. This is why self-awareness and consciousness are so critical: The more you know what's influencing your choices, the clearer your mind will be when you make them. And the more in tune with your intuition those choices will be. Just be still and ask a higher power for guidance. All will be presented to you in the reverence of silence.

The only way something can have power over you is if you surrender your own power to choose right now.

Will you walk the path of suffering, the dark trail of painful stories retold day after day? Or will you walk the path of the highest good, a road paved in peace, goodwill, and gratitude? Unconscious stories or conscious surrender? Unconscious pain or conscious peace? Unconscious hell or conscious healing? Bring your awareness to the choices you make. We often unconsciously grasp for the very things we don't want. Get crystal clear about your role in this process. Do not allow yourself to be defined by anything other than this very moment making this very choice. The only way something can have power over you is if you surrender your own power to choose right now. The choice is yours. So what will it be?

THE PATH OF HIGHEST GOOD

There is a path that's meant for you. You can feel it in your bones when you're walking along it. You feel supported, happy, and whole. You have faith that you are being led to what's meant for you. You believe in the deepest part of your being that life is unfolding for your benefit and guiding you to grow.

This path has been called by many names. It's been called the journey to enlightenment, the spiritual path, the surrendered life, and the path of highest good. All of those are accurate representations because they all point to the same truth: You are on a growth journey known as life. No matter what you call it, you are walking along a road intended for you and you alone. This road is paved with lessons, each one intricately and ornately inscribed with truth, and each one delicately placed on your path. Another conversation with Life. Another encounter with Change. Another chance with Choice.

When we walk the path with grace and humility, miracles unfold before our eyes. What we used to perceive as challenges and roadblocks are suddenly transformed into lessons that we can choose to learn—exercises that will make us stronger and more resilient, giving us everything we need to traverse the rough seas yet to come.

We walk this road blindly, feeling our way forward one step, one Change, one choice, and one experience at a time. We are not meant to know where it leads. In fact, where it leads doesn't really matter because it's not the point. It is the *path* of highest good not the *pinnacle* of highest good. We are shown our lessons by walking the path not by arriving at the destination, if there is such a thing at all. It is the willingness to walk—the choice to remain open to what life has to teach us—that matters. This is the essence of the spiritual journey. And every journey is a spiritual one because every journey mirrors back to us the unconscious parts of ourselves that we have yet to bring to light, that we have yet to heal. Every journey shows us if we are resisting or accepting Change. Every journey of consequence makes us ask life's big questions.

This, of course, is not the only way. Many folks deny their path of highest good, give up their power to choose, and ignore their opportunities to learn from Change. This is also a path—one that is often chosen in the darkness and unawareness of the unconscious mind and one that leads us further into darkness.

There's a reason why many people unconsciously choose this path. It is because they struggle to understand that life doesn't happen to them; life happens through them. We are the path and Life is the walk. Life is experienced only through Change. Things will move and expand as Life dances through us. When we defy this movement and expansion, we defy Life and thereby defy ourselves. That is why we feel so lost.

Your path of highest good unfolds through you regardless of your reluctance to see it and walk it—despite your resistance of Change. It shows up in the form of a breakup that blindsides us, the death of a close friend or family member that crushes us, or the eviction notice that brings us to our knees. These sudden shifts show us that we've been ignoring our path of highest good, that we've been defying Change. You can't ever be blindsided when you're comfortable walking the path blindly to begin with. This is easier said than done. Few people in all of human history have been fully committed to this way of life. Still, our path is ours and ours alone to claim. Our lives truly begin when we realize this truth.

My realization came in the form of an abrupt change several years ago. I'll never forget my boss calling me into his office. He uttered five simple words that took the breath from my lungs and pulled tears to my cheeks.

"We are letting you go," he said; sorrow forming in the corners of his eyes. "Someone from HR is waiting downstairs to walk you through your severance package."

Just like that, after over three years of hard work on behalf of the company, I was dismissed to discuss the particulars of leaving a job I loved but had clearly grown out of.

Hello again, Change. It's good to see you, I thought.

I was 30 years old and unemployed, struggling to find my way forward that summer, when rather than simply asking myself disempowering and deflating questions, I started asking empowering and existential ones too. *Why am I here? What is my purpose? What are my gifts? What made me feel fulfilled in the past? How can I do more of that now? What is this trying to teach me?*

The answers to those questions came to me slowly over time. They first arrived as inspiration—random thoughts that popped into my head out of nowhere. Then they appeared as doors that closed—opportunities that once felt promising or fruitful slowly began to dissipate or disappear altogether. As my situation evolved, I started to see more clearly. One day I sat down and started writing. After an hour of scribbling thoughts in a notebook, some concrete answers finally emerged. I realized that I wanted to help others learn the lessons I'd learned. I discovered that my deepest longing was to share my own struggles so people could see how I came out stronger on the other side. I came to see that my path of highest good was to help other people find theirs.

For a long time I knew this to be true about myself. I daydreamed of becoming an author and public speaker. I longed to use my life journey as an example of how to transcend one's past and seize the present moment instead. But I resisted ever pursuing this path for fear that I might fail or that others would ridicule me. I abandoned my dreams. And I lost myself in the process.

Or at least that's what I thought.

Present-day me is here to offer up another explanation: When you *feel* lost, it's not that you've really *lost* yourself; it's that you've surrendered your power to consciously choose and as a result have allowed yourself to feel unconsciously powerless. Eckhart Tolle put this beautifully when he pondered in *A New Earth*: "How can I lose something that I Am? It is impossible." This quote is the basis for this book. How can you possibly lose yourself? You simply *think* you're lost. You simply *think* you need to find your way back. You simply *think* you've gone down the wrong path. But just because you think it doesn't make it true. How can you lose your way if you *are* the way? It is impossible. The only place you are ever lost is *in your mind*.

Life, then, is about finding harmony between our inner world and outer orbit. It's an exercise in unlearning our coping mechanisms for pain, becoming aware of our reflexive reactions to Change, and making conscious choices. It's a journey of allowing yourself to crack open. It's the process of embracing pain, finding space in your heart to forgive, learning to see past the flaws in another, looking for love and letting the rest go. It is resisting only one thing: Our own resistance to the path of highest possible good.

When we give up resisting, we welcome acceptance into our life and peace into our hearts. Life flows freely when we don't get in the way. This flow leads us to a higher state of receptivity, where we are open to all of life's blessings—foreseen and unforeseen, expected and unexpected. Trusting that we are being led to what's meant for us, we become thankful and focused on faith and growth. From this state of gratitude, we progress in the direction of joy, where light governs our thoughts, feelings, and actions—and we are at one with our divinity and humanity simultaneously.

This is how we find ourselves again. We quit telling the stories of our pain. We take them off of repeat mode and rewrite them instead. We stop playing the role of the victim and we choose to be a survivor instead. We embrace Change. We let go of resentment and anger. We learn to see our own actions and the actions of others as either love or a call to love. We act empathetically, cry compassionately, and live righteously. Each moment becomes another opportunity to spread your light, to be a positive beam of energy in the darkness. Every detour becomes a doorway to something greater than we ever could've imagined for ourselves.

Change is difficult. But it's also the natural flow of life. And, while Change can sometimes be painful in both a physical or mental way, when we create stories about our pain we identify with that pain and cause suffering. This suffering creates an imbalance. The second arrow strikes us where we feel most vulnerable. When we suffer in this way, we unintentionally surrender our power to consciously choose. Giving up this sacred gift makes us feel disillusioned, powerless, and lost. When we feel lost, we feel unsafe. When we feel unsafe, we make decisions that are reckless, unconscious, and out of tune with who we are. These decisions only cause more suffering because we're acting in a way that's incongruent with our true nature. We use our own power to choose against ourselves. This is how we turn against the path of highest good.

How do you find your way back? First, you stop identifying with the pain of your past. You quit telling yourself stories about how horrific or painful it was. You refuse to be a victim any longer. No amount of pity or wallowing will change what happened. We must do the work to accept what can't be changed. Next, you embrace your path of highest good in the present. This means using the light of your awareness to make more conscious choices that will support and nourish you, that will help you accept your opportunities to grow. The final step is to stop resisting Change in the future. When something unexpected happens that triggers you, do not react. Learn to lean on your faith. Trust that what happens is for your ultimate benefit even if you can't fathom how. Accept every unforeseen plot twist and embrace every obstacle as an impetus to evolve. This is what it means to heal. This is what it means to find peace. This is what it means to truly know Change. We do it by following the **RACE Model for Change**:

- **Resist** one thing only: Your resistance to Change.
- **Accept** what you can't Change so you may let go.
- **Choose** to Change what you can by reclaiming your power to choose.
- **Embrace** Change by remaining open to it in the future.

The **RACE Model for Change** shows us not just how to embrace Change, but how to completely transform our relationship with it. The rest of the book will follow this framework step by step.

In the **Resisting** section, I'll walk you through how I resisted some of my own experiences with Change and what they had to teach me, revealing how they felt and what I realize in looking back at these learning assignments with peace and perspective.

In the **Accepting** section, I'll show you how I learned to let go of those painful memories that I couldn't Change. We'll practice radical acceptance together, and I'll provide you with exercises, activities, and reflections that will help you to forgive and be grateful.

After we accept the past we'll move on to the **Choosing** section, where I'll share some tools and techniques for how to make choices that support your path of highest good.

Once we choose to invest in ourselves we'll journey into the **Embracing** section, where I'll share some wisdom and mindset shifts for how to stay open to life and be receptive to Change so you can stay on the path of highest good.

You've been guided to this book for a reason. If you've been looking for a sign, wishing for clarity, or hoping for direction, this is it. Your life is speaking to you through the words on these pages. Should you choose to listen, you will rediscover the truth of who you are. Should you accept this assignment, you will awaken the parts of you that you thought were lost forever. A homecoming of the soul awaits those who are brave enough to choose this path. All you have to do is give yourself permission to embrace it.

From the pain of resistance to the peace of acceptance, and from the power of choosing to the bliss of being open to life, this is a voyage of resilience and redemption, fear and forgiveness, judgment and joy. Follow this model and you will always find your way back home to you. Choose to embark on this journey and you will learn to befriend Change. Choose the path of highest good laid out for you and you will finally realize that *it's good to see me again*.

2
Resisting

NOT MEASURING UP

The Kings Dominion amusement park near Richmond, Virginia, was like heaven to me as a four-year-old boy. I spent a day there with my dad and two older sisters—one of the only outings we ever had just the four of us.

Standing there at the foot of a roller coaster, I gawked at how massive it appeared, how it roared with a menacing growl, the ground shaking every time its screaming passengers flew directly over our heads.

"I want to go on that one, Dad!" I said, pointing my short, stubby arm at the steel giant that towered above.

"Okay, Son. We'll go with you. Let's get in line over here," he said, grabbing my hand and escorting me into the proper queue. We waited anxiously for the better part of an hour before it was our turn to board the ride. As we neared the front, I hopped out of my stroller, wanting to stand tall and proud to board my very first roller coaster. The ride attendant eyed me up and down, realizing just how young I was. He directed me to stand by a stick, assessing my exact height and comparing it to the minimum required for the ride. Then he glanced at my dad and shook his head, adding, "Sorry, today's not your day, Buddy."

I missed it by one inch. Still, I wasn't allowed to ride the roller coaster. My dreams were dashed in an instant. My sister, Michele, stayed back with me as my oldest sister, Jennifer, and my father, Brett, rode the ride. My giddiness instantly subsided to gloom, and my gloom soon subsided to frustration. As my dad and sister returned, I hopped back into the stroller and buckled myself in, not saying a word.

We stayed at the park for several more hours, but I said very little. No attempt to coax me was successful. No amount of children's amusements could distract me from the disappointment. My expectations had been too high, and my body unfortunately fell short. The experience just wasn't what I wanted it to be; it wasn't what I envisioned in my head. It didn't measure up.

And neither did I.

GREAT EXPECTATIONS

In the amusement park of life, there are many times where you don't get to ride the roller coaster of your choice. You might not get that big promotion you think you deserve. You might lose a love you thought would last forever. You might get into an accident that changes the trajectory of your entire life. In the end, it doesn't matter which coaster we climb, it's how we make the most of the ride.

Expectations will eat you alive if you let them. They will convince you of how your life *should've* turned out, or what *could've* happened if only you'd acted sooner. The greater your expectations, the greater your disappointment will be when they don't come to fruition. Life falls short—even if just by a hair—when you walk the path of highest good with specific requirements. Things don't quite measure up when you go through life with the rigidity of your expectations. This rigidity is the essence of resistance. These discrepancies give rise to our disappointments. How can you embrace life's plot twists if you've already written the plot for yourself? How can you grow if you don't think there's anything for you to learn? How can you find fulfillment if it shows up as a breakup instead of a wedding, or a pink slip instead of a promotion? You can't. And you won't. Because you think you know better. Until you don't.

THE TUG OF WAR

Life only asks one thing of us: To be present for each and every moment for as many moments as we are fortunate enough to receive. Ignoring this singular request is how resistance is born. Resistance is nothing more than the refusal to accept one moment changing into another, to believe that one moment isn't acceptable as it is and to think it should be swapped for another moment instead. It reveals itself as a defiance of reality, a rebellion against something that can't be changed, an insistence of how things should be, the rejection of the facts in favor of a story.

He shouldn't have died at such a young age, we think with cocktail in hand, knowing full well that any one of us could die at any moment. We forget just how fortunate we are to live at all.

I'll never find love again, we convince ourselves after a breakup, knowing that if we truly hold that belief close to our hearts, we won't ever get hurt again because we simply won't let ourselves try. We forget the power of our intention to shape our reality.

I can't believe she betrayed me like that, we cry in a state of victimization, with the unconscious understanding that at some point in our lives someone has said the exact same thing about us. We forget that we're just as human as the next person.

These stories all have one thing in common: Their fear of allowing the present moment to be utterly as it is.

Life feels like a tug of war for those who can't accept the truth of the present moment. You keep pushing and pulling, resisting and denying, until you're thrown from your position and dragged through the mud. It all starts with an idea in your head of how things should be. When this expectation isn't met, you feel slighted by the Universe. You think: *Why can't things be the way I imagined them? There must be something wrong with me*, you falsely conclude. But the only thing wrong is the way you're showing up for circumstances in front of you. In any given moment your inability to accept reality is directly proportional to your lack of faith in the Universe. You would rather be right than simply let go and let God. You would rather perpetuate drama than be at peace.

What you're really saying, though, is that deep down you don't think you deserve better. If you really felt that way, you would let things unfold as they are because you'd know in your heart of hearts that you'd find your way forward no matter what happens.

You might feel like your heart's shattered into a thousand pieces yet somehow, some way, you will be put back together. You will be raised up to light and shown how strong you are. You will be golden.

Instead, we prefer to tug and tug and tug. We insist and control and demand that things happen a certain way. When they don't, we are put in a state of incontrovertible shock, dismay, and overwhelm. This is what gives rise to our reluctance to accept reality. When we avoid the truth of a situation, we amplify its gravitas, causing suffering in our hearts and our lives. We are thrown by the tug of war each time. The more suffering we endure, the more we avoid or resist, since ultimately all resistance is an avoidance of the perceived pain of Change—a denial of the lesson laid out for us on our path.

To break this tug of war, we must relinquish how we think things should be, and embrace how they are instead. We must accept what arises as it comes and do our best to live in a state of nonresistance, never trying to preserve a moment or protect ourselves from it.

We can drop the rope or prepare for the burns. It's up to us.

THE THREE REASONS

Throughout my life, I've suffered because I was afraid of Change. While Change showed up in many forms, my resistance manifested in a distinct pattern. Based on that pattern, I've surmised three primary reasons we resist:

RESISTING

1. We want to protect ourselves from feeling bad.
2. We want to preserve what makes us feel good.
3. We combine the first two in an attempt to preserve and protect ourselves.

All three scenarios cause suffering because they are each the mental equivalent of lying down in a river and expecting the rapids to come to a halt. The current of life can't be stopped. Whether or not you want to float downstream, the stream will flow regardless. When you resist, you remain One With Self: You put your own agenda and expectations ahead of what may actually be best for you. When you relinquish, you remain One With Life: You cast aside your vision to trust in a grander one instead. Choose the former and you will drown in the current. Choose the latter and you will float and flourish.

More times than I'd care to admit, I've been the guy standing in the middle of the river trying to stop it from flowing. I've felt the sheer magnitude of what it's like to drown in suffering. I stood tall even as the bedrock threatened to give out from under me, and I dug my heels in further. *You're not going to get me*, I snarled in my head. *I'll show you.*

There are several problems with this approach. One, it's unsustainable; there's no way you can outlast the everlasting. Two, it's incredibly, undeniably, excruciatingly painful. There's really no describing or justifying how foolish it is to try to tame the river of life. You are one with it. When you try to separate yourself from it, you abdicate your seat of personal power. Lastly, it accomplishes nothing. The Universe only amplifies your energy. If you spend all of your energy resisting, you're essentially telling the Universe to give you more things to resist. Resisting the current of change only makes that change more difficult to accept when it finally washes over you.

Over and over again, I've failed to accept my life as it is without judgment or fear. I've given into the allure of resistance, thinking that I could protect myself from the bad feelings and preserve myself by holding tight to the good ones. But the more I dismissed or detained the present moment, the more I felt myself slipping away. When it comes to your resistance, you only have one option available to you: Be willing to let go or be willing to get washed away in the process.

A MILLION UNCONSCIOUS CHOICES

Until we accept that we are free to let go and let life be as it is without our tugging and separation, our insistence and resistance, we'll feel like we've lost our way again and again. We'll act on our negative narratives. We'll give over our power to consciously choose. We'll make a million unconscious choices.

An unconscious choice is a diversion from the path of highest good, a decision to substitute something for the experience of Change. It's not *what* you substitute that's the problem, though we often reach for substitutes that are risky and bad for our health and well-being, only complicating matters further. It's the act of turning to a substitute *in and of itself* that's disconcerting. It signals that you're only able to be present for your life if you're able to control all the variables. You demonstrate that you lack the courage to sit with Change. This lack of courage is the crux of the dilemma. Change is a fundamental part of the human experience. It is impossible to outrun. To avoid this fact is folly. Life doesn't care about your willingness to live it. You can either live your life or your life will live you.

Over the years, I've witnessed countless detours away from the path of highest good. One guy I know experienced the unconscious choice of a loved one firsthand. Let's call him Calvin. When Calvin was just five years old, he was the victim of molestation at the hands of his older sister. Calvin resisted the reality of his trauma for many years, repressing the memory deep inside. When it finally came to the surface, he felt angry, disgusted, and betrayed. *Why would my own sister do this to me?* He wondered. A somber sense of embarrassment washed over him. Worried that anyone who found out would pity or ridicule him, Calvin carried around this dark secret for years on end with no one to talk to. As a result of his unconscious choice to stay silent, he learned to bury his needs and resist his feelings. He suffered immensely.

Another person I know, whom I've dubbed Jack, lost his mom suddenly when he was just 18 years old. As a college freshman at the time, Jack spent many late nights in bars and clubs binge drinking and dancing the night away. This kept Jack emotionally numb, and he was able to get by for a while. But without the tools to properly cope, Jack fell into a despondent state and began drinking even more. Jack was a straight-A student but his grades plummeted in the semester following the death of his mother. Between the drinking and the stories in his head that told him *it's all your fault*, he never really gave himself a chance to process his grief. He struggled to bounce back for years after the loss.

And then there is a girl I'll refer to as Natalie. Natalie struggled to love herself. She never quite felt *good enough* as she was; she always felt that she was somehow *less than* others around her. Her shame manifested in myriad ways but her coping mechanism was always the same: Lots and lots of sex. She boasted of her sexual conquests and remarked at how many guys told her she was beautiful on dating apps, social media, and, of course, between the sheets. These hits of instant gratification and validation were temporary highs that stoked her ego. But they would inevitably wear off, leaving Natalie feeling inadequate and isolated. Eventually, Natalie would find herself on another app talking to another guy and the cycle would begin again. Natalie spent years in this pattern, feeling emptier and emptier inside and chasing the worthiness that she failed to realize she already possessed.

I watched these harrowing stories unfold and witnessed unconscious coping mechanisms get activated in one hurtful situation after another. Burying emotions, binge drinking, and having meaningless sex were examples of how Calvin, Jack, and Natalie processed the pain they didn't know how to feel and the Change they didn't know how to process. Truth is we've all been there; we've all been a Calvin or Jack or Natalie at one point or another. Whether it's as innocent as a glass of wine after a tough day at work or as intense as a full-blown drug dependency, we numb, avoid, and bury our pain in ways big and small each and every day. Many of us don't know the first thing about processing Change because we were never shown how. We're stunted from an emotional standpoint. We might appear as grown adults on the outside, but our emotional growth lags far behind. We don't sit still long enough to listen to ourselves. We haven't cultivated a relationship with our inner world. We can "solve for x" but we can't get over our exes. We can find the square root of a number but we can't get to the root of our emotions. We can define words but we can't define feelings. That's why, like a hand recoiling from a flame, we run away from Change at the first sign of discomfort. We don't know what else to do except attempt to escape.

Resistance creates an alternate reality in our minds—one where we unintentionally grasp onto the second arrow of suffering and pull it deeper into our hearts. This alternate reality is flippantly fabricated in order to fulfill the promises of our expectations. The more we choose to invest in this proxy perspective, the more detours we make, since we are acting on a version of reality that does not exist. These choices compound over time until we arrive at a point where we don't understand what's happening around us or within us.

In the end, our detours are unconscious behavior patterns that are primarily driven by fear of and resistance to Change. These detours have repercussions of their own—ripples of consequence that ebb into every corner of our lives—but at their core they are driven by the same thing: Wanting life to be different than it is.

When Change shows up and triggers you, you act unconsciously—that is, without awareness. Reflexively, you do everything you can to avoid feeling the pain that's arisen. You don't even realize you're doing it, but you start acting in a way that subverts your best interests. You rationalize your decision to reach for whatever coping mechanism is available. *Anything's better than feeling this way*, you think. You're not concerned with the consequences anymore because you aren't acting with awareness and intention. This is why our stories become so difficult to unravel. What starts out as resistance to Change warps into a complex piece of machinery that we use to cope with what we believe we can't handle.

This is one of the main dilemmas of life. We'll do absolutely everything at our disposal—use up every choice available to us, exhaust every resource at our fingertips—but we won't allow ourselves to actually trust Change. Ask yourself, *When was the last time I let my heart break? When was the last time I allowed myself to get hurt? When was the last time I sat with my emotional pain instead of dismissing it or acting on it?*

Resistance is a fall from grace. It is a discarding of our faith in the Universal guidance available to us at any time. When we fail to believe that—no matter how difficult it may seem—life is unfolding for our benefit, we fall into darkness. Refusing to accept our learning assignments is how we turn away from the path that's meant for us. When you walk away from this path, you walk away from yourself. This is what makes you feel lost. You'll sacrifice anything not to experience Change. But the most painful sacrifice of all is when you sacrifice yourself to do it.

Your soul can never be at peace while you are at war with Change. Resistance intensifies the storms of life. It creates hurricanes of the heart, tsunamis of the soul, firestorms within the fiber of our being. It robs us of our peace. How do I know? Because Calvin, Jack, and Natalie aren't real. Their stories are actually mine.

THE BIRTH OF A FLAME

"No, don't wear that—wear the black turtleneck instead," my sister, Michele, said while helping me get dressed for an excursion to the Kennedy Space Center at Cape Canaveral with our mom over Christmas break one year.

"But I want to wear my Mickey Mouse shirt," I said, frowning.

"Do what I say or I'll tell mom your little secret," she said. I threw on the turtleneck and began sobbing.

"Please don't tell mom!" I said, pleading with her. I was desperate for our mother not to find out that I was different from all the other little boys.

"It looks better on you than that stupid Mickey Mouse shirt anyway," Michele said, brushing aside my frantic plea. I was no older than nine at the time and that Disney shirt was my favorite piece of clothing—a symbol of innocence long lost but to which I so desperately clung.

I was far too young to understand that I could stand up for myself. I didn't know that I should have owned my truth. I hadn't yet realized that I was gay. All I knew was that my sister witnessed another young boy and I innocently and curiously exploring each other's bodies on the playground just the year prior. I was petrified and ashamed of anyone else finding out—especially our mom or dad. So I let Michele blackmail me. I thought I was forced to oblige all of her demands lest my secret get spilled.

But I wasn't the only one with a secret to hide.

Michele was nine years old when I was born. Our parents gave her the opportunity to select my middle name. She chose Robert, after the boy down the street on whom she had a crush. By the time I turned four and Michele turned 13, her life had been completely turned upside down. Our parents had separated and finalized a pretty brutal divorce. Our mom revealed to Michele that my dad was not her biological father. Michele was never the same again after that. Neither was our family. But I didn't have a clue what any of it meant. Michele and I were absolutely inseparable. I remember she used to play with me and we'd laugh uncontrollably for hours. She was a sweet soul riddled with crippling emotional trauma that the tides of Change had cast upon her. With me she was carefree and seemed genuinely happy.

One winter night when I was five years old, Michele and I were curled up on the couch watching a movie at home when things took a turn into darkness. It was at that moment that my own 14-year-old sister reached down my pants and touched my private parts. She then took my hand and pulled it behind my back, quietly guiding it down the front of her jeans. Michele whispered in my ear to be quiet. Dad was in the next room and within yelling distance, but I obeyed, bewildered by the moment while simultaneously not wanting to upset her. Queasiness washed over me. A knot formed in my throat. A fire formed in my heart.

There are moments when I can still feel her skin on mine. Almost three decades later, the tinge of her hand tugging my arm gives me chills. I didn't know what was happening, but I knew it wasn't supposed to. Even then in my developing mind I knew that a line was crossed. I could feel the violation like a knife cutting through bone. A sacred bond of trust sliced in two. The birth of a flame.

Michele and I never spoke about that night, though there were times I looked into her eyes and saw the war that waged within her, the fire of suffering that ignited my own. She knew what she had done.

While that was the only time anything of that nature ever happened between us, the sensations were scorched into my memory the way electricity scars wood. Its veins were black and branch-like, running thick and deep through the core of my body. The threats in the years that followed only pushed the branding iron deeper; scarring me at a level so close to my core that at times it felt like wildfire flowed through me.

I repressed the memory of the molestation for over 25 years after it happened, locking it away in a cage in my subconscious mind where it lay dormant, out of my active awareness and mental reach. I unconsciously resisted feeling the pain and trauma until Michele suddenly died of a drug overdose in 2018. After her death, the memories came flooding back, reigniting the flame within me.

I was confused, perplexed, and puzzled. *How could she do that to me?* I pondered, grasping for an excuse for the inexcusable. No matter how hard I tried, I failed to understand how a 14-year-old girl could sexually assault her own five-year-old brother. I felt violated, defiled, and desecrated. The age-old story that asked: *Did I do something to deserve this?* Played over and over in my mind. The pain was palpable, like a cloud of ash that lingered in the air after she passed. I sat with that cloud for months before I allowed myself to go to the mouth of the volcano. And dive in.

HOT ANGUISH

When you experience something deeply hurtful, like what happened between Michele and I, the sensory information from the experience feels like it's burned onto your bones. You can't forget how it felt. You are forced to relive the memory over and over. It feels like it's become a part of who you are. You feel degraded, unsafe, insecure, and taken advantage of. The embers of a firestorm linger within. It feels like no amount of time will help you heal.

This, of course, is not fundamentally true. Healing is always possible for those who are willing to welcome it into their heart. It doesn't matter how many times you were brandished with the iron. It doesn't matter how large the inferno or how hot the flames burned. All that matters is that you want to heal more than you want to keep the fire alive within. And how do we stoke the flames inside? We tell ourselves stories about how horrific it was, how unfathomable it feels, how we'll never, ever recover.

Our stories are powerful and enduring. They bleed down into the marrow of our being and sit there untouched for years or even decades. The stories we create about the victimization we've endured are tinder to a fire, fanning the embers within to blaze once more. Our stories drain us physically and mentally because they require energy to sustain. *How could you do this to me?* We ask our perpetrator accusingly and rhetorically over and over in our mind. "Can you believe that happened to me?" We question in seek of pity. In the end, our stories are nothing more than a misdirected use of attention. Underneath what you tell yourself about the event is the reality of the event itself, the ephemeral elemental data that was raised to your awareness. It's the soft touch of a sister desecrating her oath of protection. It's the flat line on a hospital monitor that signals the absence of presence. It's the moisture that forms on our cheeks after we hear, "I just can't do this anymore," or, "I think we need to see other people."

You can't hold a fire in your heart and expect it not to burn you. Release the flame and you will begin to heal.

Below the data of the event is an even deeper truth: Our pain is just an indicator of how deeply we can love. Our false, fearful stories are cheap, conditional substitutes for what we truly seek. Our cup of love runs dry and we become desperate to be quenched. But we will remain parched until we stand up and believe *enough is enough*, until we choose differently, until we release the resistance.

In order to release resentment, bitterness, and hatred you need to actively replace them with compassion, acceptance, and peace. No amount of anger or sadness will allow you to go back and change the past. Give yourself permission to remember it through the lens of love so that you can own your future. You can't hold a fire in your heart and expect it not to burn you. Release the flame and you will begin to heal. Surround yourself with the safety, security, and trust you crave and you will surmount your pain and rediscover peace once more.

KISSES THROUGH THE PHONE

The screams were deafening. My mom's shrieks bellowed inside her sedan as she cursed a tractor trailer that barreled past us on the highway. She pulled over to the shoulder, ran around to the other side of the car, whipped open the passenger side door, and frantically began checking me for any sign of blood or injury. She hugged me close and then grabbed me by my shoulders while she looked me in my eyes. "I'm so glad you're okay, Sweetie!" Tears were streaming down her cheeks as she spoke. "I don't know what I would have done if anything bad had happened to you."

"Don't worry, Mommy. I'm okay," I said, shaken up by the shocking turn of events.

It was a bone-chilling winter's day—one of those days after a snowstorm that's unnervingly serene. My mom trekked through the weather to pick me up. On the ride back to her house, an 18-wheeler truck was speeding as it passed us on the highway. The velocity of the vehicle broke loose a chunk of snow and ice the size of a human head from the roof of the truck, sending it hurtling toward the windshield of my mom's car, nearly shattering it in the process.

It was anything but the routine weekend trip to visit my mom. A couple of weeks and a new windshield later, a tractor-trailer of a different kind hit us. This time it nearly shattered my heart.

"Do you know where Mickey Mouse lives?" My mom asked, easing into the news.

"Of course I do. He lives in Florida," I said, hoping she was planning a vacation for us.

"That's right! Great job, Honey. Mickey is actually going to be our new neighbor," she said, leaving me to wonder what she meant.

"Does that mean you and Mr. Bill are moving to Florida?" I asked, referring to my mom and her second husband. This time, I was the one with emotion welling up in my eyes.

"Yes, Sweetheart, it does. I know it's further away, but when you come to visit, we can see each other for longer. Mommy will make sure she sees you as often as she can." She pulled me in close and we embraced for what felt like an hour.

Thus began my first long-distance relationship—the one I had with my mom. I spent the next decade of my life flying back and forth to see her a couple of times each year during holidays and summers off from school. In between trips, my mom sent me letters, postcards, and gifts, and we talked on the phone for hours on end. We ended each call with vocal kisses—symbols of love expressed across telephone wires and thousands of miles. She always knew how to calm me down and comfort me when times got tough or when I got anxious. And I felt that way pretty often.

The emotional roller coaster typically went something like this: I flew down to Florida from Maryland and had an incredible time with my mom. We went to amusement parks and the beach. We went shopping and had fancy dinners out on the town. We drove to Tampa and Miami and Orlando. All was well because I was content to just spend quality time with my mom like every other normal kid. As the days turned into minutes and minutes turned to seconds, I dreaded the impending separation.

And then the time ran out.

The flight back was always the worst. I was typically in an inconsolable state of disbelief and grief. On a few different occasions, the flight attendant saw how distraught I was upon leaving Florida and let me call my mom from the phone on the plane. Then the long-distance relationship and equally long-winded phone conversations started fresh once more.

After each return to Baltimore, I was despondent and disheartened, taking several weeks to recover emotionally. I didn't want to do anything. I didn't want to talk to anyone. I was completely consumed by the idea of reuniting with my mom. Eventually, my mom and dad agreed upon a date for me to go back down and the ticket was purchased—and my hope restored. I remember counting down the days for months in advance, looking forward to when I'd get to see her again. I got so excited for each trip that I couldn't sleep the night before my flight. But I wasn't concerned about sleep. My singular concern was getting on that plane and arriving in Florida as soon as humanly possible. Upon landing, my mom picked me up from the airport and I ran into her arms.

And thus the roller coaster began again all the same.

TORN IN TWO

I spent years in this vicious cycle, burying my deep-seated feelings of rejection and my need for closeness. The only thing that made me feel like I could exist peacefully was by starting another countdown for when I'd see her again. Then things seemed fine.

But they were most certainly not fine.

I was profoundly hurt and felt torn between two worlds—the

one at home in Maryland with my father and the one in Florida with my mother. I couldn't fathom why my mom would choose to move a thousand miles away from me after being able to share custody with my dad and see me every other weekend.

Looking back now, I know my mom was just as torn apart as I was. I recognize that she remarried and was merely fulfilling her marital duties to her husband by following him to another state. I see that she was doing the best she could. I am cognizant that, while she was not directly culpable, she made a choice. And, despite it all, she deserves my forgiveness.

But it's also important to respect the feelings I felt as a result of her choice. I felt shunned. I felt cast aside and pushed away. I felt inadequate. I felt abandoned. This is how I learned to model a relationship and attach to others. This is how I learned to internalize the feeling of love.

Throughout my 20s, I ended up in several long-distance relationships that left me just as brokenhearted and bewildered as when I flew home from Florida after seeing my mom. There was the first guy I ever loved who moved to Tampa and wanted to try to make it work long distance. There was a guy who lived in Baltimore that I met while on a trip back home to visit a friend. There was a guy I met on Fire Island who lived in Washington D.C. And there was an old college friend I reconnected with in New York that lived in Chicago. No matter which state I was in, long-distance love seemed to find me.

There's a reason for that.

Truthfully, I found some solace in the familiarity of a long-distance love because I learned to cope with being torn in two—with constantly wondering when I would see my mom or, later, my significant other again. In reality, I sought out the same pain that I had known from all those years going to and from Florida. Because I was identified with the painful story that I told myself that said, *You don't deserve anyone closer*, that I didn't get to feel love up close. Truth is, I knew how to deny that ache and bury it as deep within me as it could go.

It's no coincidence that relationship patterns repeat themselves in your life if you don't notice the underlying cause and bring it to light. The script keeps playing out and you continue to recreate the dysfunctional dynamic, hoping desperately to change the outcome this time around. But the result is always the same because it's a self-fulfilling prophecy of pain and shame. The only way out of this real-life *Groundhog Day* is to heal the hurt caused by the original wound—to acknowledge that your feelings and needs are valid, and no one else's choices can ever take that away from you. If you honor your soul in this way and decide to choose differently than you have before, you will find your footing again. Only then can you reclaim your power. Only then can you reorient yourself back on the path of highest good. Only then can you break the cycle once and for all.

After so many heartbreaks and so much time spent reopening old wounds, I decided that enough was enough. I realized that if I learned to interpret distance as love, I could unlearn it, too. I realized that the conditioning could be undone. I could replace the insecure impressions left in my mind and choose secure ones instead.

Once you stop living the script you've written for yourself, you'll finally have the space in your heart for the Universe to write a new story for you. This time it won't be rooted in fear—it'll be rooted in love. This time you'll have a peaceful ending. This time your kisses will be true and real—and not just through the phone.

THE FINAL GOODBYE

In my mind, I can still see her glistening alabaster skin. The mid-afternoon sun is beaming through sheer hospital curtains before it catches the reflection of my tears on her arm. I'm holding her hands in both of mine, but they're clammy and cool—and losing warmth by the second. Life has left her body and I'm trying so desperately to summon it back to her. I'm blowing in my cupped hands to warm hers up as if we've come inside from a cold winter's day. I'm whispering in her ear, "I'll love you forever, Mom" and begging her, "Please don't leave me" as if she can heed my request from the other side. I'm doing everything I can to rebel against the truth of her departure.

But she's gone where there is no return. She's passed on from this realm. She's dead. And so my sobs take the place of her breath, my body rocks and writhes and shakes in the absence of her movement, my tears fall like rain and become one with her pale white complexion below.

Loving my mom was a waterfall—emotions overflowing the vessels meant to contain them. In an instant, I recall poolside tears on a childhood visit to Florida where I threw a temper tantrum and refused to leave her side. And I was so mean to my mother that it made her cry. Seeing her get emotional broke me immediately, and I went to hug her and apologize. "I'm sorry, Mommy," I said, wiping away the tears from her face. "I don't want to leave. I hate being so far apart."

"It breaks my heart too, Chris, but we're never really apart," she said as she drew a heart on my bare chest with her finger. "I'm always in here. No amount of distance or time can take that away from us. You'll always be my baby boy." We embraced and cried together a little more.

Another flash and another memory surfaces. I remember bedside tears on a hospital visit near the end where she scribbled "you are beautiful" hurriedly on a memo pad as she smiled at me, eyes welling up with pride. She was admiring me in the only way she could after her tracheotomy—in black pen on a yellow legal pad. She somehow sensed we didn't have much longer together.

When I think of my mom, I still think of moisture. I reminisce about days by the pool, weekends at the beach, and trips to the water park. I remember watching Florida afternoon thunderstorms with her on the porch. I remember running through sprinklers in the front yard while screaming at the top of our lungs. I remember singing our way through the car wash, watching the bubbles fly across the windshield and making back and forth motions with our arms to mimic them. I'll never forget her wet kisses on the cheek, laughing until we cried, and crying until we hugged. It's these moments that overcome me with tears of joy.

I also remember the war of addiction that waged within her. I recall dumping her bottles of booze down the drain. I remember flushing her packs of cigarettes down the toilet. I can still hear myself asking, "What's in that cup, Mommy?" It's these moments that overcome me with tears of pain.

If those tears are a measurement of our love, I loved her deeper than the ocean, more fiercely than a hurricane, with the loyalty of the tides. Though the waves have grown weaker over the years, one thing remains certain: My love for her never stops flowing. As long as my heart beats, I will cry for her. As long as my lungs breathe, a piece of her lives on. As long as the waves break on the shore, I'll think of her once more.

Always.

HASTA LA GRIEFSTA, BABY

I just couldn't bring myself to do it.

I stared down at my flight itinerary, pondering my next move for the better part of an hour. I knew what I should do. I knew what the wise decision was. I knew what my family wanted me to do.

And I did the complete opposite instead.

Six days after my mom passed away, my grandfather on my dad's side had a massive heart attack and died. This second shockwave of grief rippled through my family like a tidal wave, trouncing everything in its path.

Except for my New Year's Eve plans.

Several weeks prior, I booked a trip to Washington D.C. to ring in the New Year with friends. And then Change showed up twice in one week and left me bewildered and off balance. I couldn't think clearly and I was paralyzed by what otherwise would have been a clear choice. To me, though, it was anything but. As an 18-year-old boy, I didn't understand the repercussions of my actions. I was in complete denial that my mom and grandpa were gone. I thought it would be silly to cancel my trip to go to a funeral.

It was simultaneously the gravest unconscious decision I've ever made and the biggest act of self-betrayal I've ever committed. I cast aside my grieving family and resisted my own opportunity to mourn for a night out on the town in the nation's capital. I fought my feelings with bottle after bottle of champagne, drowning my sorrow until it was buried deep within. Worst of all, not wanting to believe that both of them were really gone, I robbed myself of my own opportunity to properly say goodbye, to dignify their lives and grieve the loss of two major loving figures in my life. In short, I ran away. I knew that watching them get buried would make it all permanent. Once that happened, it could never be taken back. But neither could the decision I made. I thought I could outrun grief, but it knew better.

LOVE WITH NOWHERE TO GO

I didn't realize she was gone until two weeks later.

I picked up the phone and dialed her number like I had a thousand times before. It rang until the answering machine finally clicked on. "Sorry, we can't come to the phone right now, but if you could please leave your…" The sound of her voice cascaded over me for the first time since she passed, making landfall like a hurricane. Her voice trailed off as the phone slipped from my hand, falling to the warm and unforgiving sidewalk below. My knees met the pavement soon thereafter as my eyes overflowed with the agony of her absence.

That's the power of Change: One second, you're on your way to class or work or the grocery store and the next, you're at a red light or in the bathroom or on a walkway in tears. Then the flashbacks flooded in. I was transported back to that conversation I had in the kitchen with my mom one Thanksgiving. A second goes by and in a flash another memory surfaces. I see the two of us in her community pool doing handstands and tossing a beach ball. Another flash, another memory. This time, I'm a little kid opening presents by the tree on Christmas day. This particular flashback is so vivid in my mind, I can feel the carpet on my bare legs, see the wrapping paper glistening in the sunlight, and smell the verdant scent of pine from a candle burning nearby—my mom's attempt to turn her Florida home into a winter wonderland. It's utterly surreal to mentally travel to another time and place when that person was right there next to you, smiling and breathing and alive as can be when you know they're gone forever.

Grief is complicated, yet simple. Grief is the perplexing and curious feeling that you've lost a part of yourself. The weight of all of your expectations for the future gathers in your gut and forms a knot in your throat. Breakups cause grief. Layoffs cause grief. Deaths cause grief. Something must feel lost in order for grief to swoop in to fill the void.

This is a fallacy, of course—another story we tell ourselves. The loss we feel is really just the love we'll never get to express. It's birthdays and holidays spent carrying on without that person. It's the cards and texts that'll never get sent. It's hugs and kisses and comfort we'll never get to share. It's all of the unspent energy ricocheting back at you through time and space. That love washes over you like a cascading wall of water full of *could've beens* and *should've beens*. Until you feel disoriented, paralyzed, and numb.

Grief is a reminder of how deeply you can love; it's there to show you that underneath all of that pain, there's a part of you that just wants to be understood. And that part of you is pure and unbridled love. Grief is your heart's emergency brake reminding you to slow down and savor this moment, and each moment hereafter, because time is precious and limited. Grief is the opposite of gratitude; it's when you love someone or something so much that you can't fathom the reality of not having them in your life. So you cling to how you think things should be instead of the way they are.

I lost my mother and grandfather just six days apart, and it seemed like my life was turned upside down. It felt like a huge chasm had opened up within my heart, leaving me vulnerable, exposed, and overwhelmed. In reality, I was feeling the collective love for both of them coalescing inside of me. There wasn't an abyss in my heart once occupied by their love; there was an ocean of it that formed in their honor, a monument to the depth of my admiration and respect for both of them. I just hadn't yet recognized it. I was resisting my own love and didn't even know it. The only task that remained was to feel it.

RESISTING

NUMB AND NUMBER

"I'm so sorry to do this, but you need to leave right now. My boyfriend will be home any second," I said hurriedly as I ushered a random guy to my apartment door at 4 a.m. "Are you serious?" He asked. "You're messing with me, right?" But I couldn't have been more serious, and I couldn't have cared less.

"No, you seriously need to leave right now." I said, not giving in. I wanted my bed to myself, after all. He walked out into the hallway, looked back at me with a grimace of pure disgust, and vanished down the stairs. I listened for the sound of the front door closing two floors below. Upon hearing it slam, I let out a huge sigh of relief, closed my apartment door, and went to sleep.

There was no boyfriend coming. I didn't have a boyfriend at the time. I went out on a Friday night, brought a guy home, and after we hooked up wanted nothing to do with him. So I made up a story that I thought would repulse him to the point of not wanting to stick around. It worked.

I wish I could say this was an isolated incident. I wish I could say I never acted out in this way. I wish I could say I was able to look at that guy in his beautiful face and apologize. But that's not how this story goes.

My 20s were spent numbing my shame with sex. Lots and lots of random sex. With guys I would never see—or want to see—again. At first, it was kind of like a game. I'd go out, have way too much to drink, and try to talk to as many cute guys as possible to see which one would want to go home with me. Most nights I was successful. Usually-sloppy, rarely-enjoyable, typically-forgettable, sometimes-safe sex would ensue. At first this was enough to make me hopeful I'd find the right guy for me. *If I'm worthy of sex then I must be worthy of love*, I thought. Cringe worthy, I know. Leasing out your self-worth to other people is a sure-fire way to end up emotionally bankrupt. And that's exactly how I felt after having lots of empty and meaningless sex.

Here's the thing about casual sex: Some people can keep it casual and actually be okay with that. Others like me just can't. I always craved something more, and I thought that if I could get a guy to hook up with me that I would easily be able to parlay that into a relationship. But that never actually came to fruition because why would it? I was jumping to home base before I even got a chance at an at-bat.

After sleeping with well over a hundred guys, the revolving door of my 20s came roaring back around to hit me in the rear. This time, it was especially painful. I had compounded the same shame I had tried so very hard to numb, resist, and avoid. Then it all came crashing down on me. Not only did I think I wasn't loveable, now my voice of shame inside gave me plenty of reasons to believe it. *You're washed up. You're a hand-me-down that no one wants. You're that guy he slept with one time who's kind of a mess. You're a slut.* Worse than any label or shame story, I wasn't being true to myself.

I waited to lose my virginity until I was with my first boyfriend. I thought it was incredibly special to have held out for someone with whom I was in a committed relationship. I never envisioned myself having sex outside of the confines of a monogamous bond, let alone that I'd sleep with dozens of random men. When the dust finally settled just before I turned 30 years old, I looked around and didn't recognize myself anymore. Who was this person that was offering himself up freely to undeserving, unreliable men that hadn't earned my trust? Surely that couldn't be me. Sadly, it was.

What started out as an exploration of my sexuality turned into my coping mechanism of choice after my mom's death. Then it developed into a full-blown habit driven by my shame. Before I knew it, I was just going through the motions because I had done it so many times. I was desperate to feel something—*anything*—even if it hurt me in the end. At least then I could focus on that pain instead of the endless ache of missing my mom.

That's what happens when you let a powerful negative belief like shame take over your life. You don't even realize that you're acting on the idea that you aren't deserving or worthy of more than what you're settling for. It seems like you're bending the rules a little bit for the sake of fun. It certainly was fun at times. I'm not going to lie and act like I didn't enjoy some of the sex I had or the fact that I was able to land some of the guys I did. But the ego boost would always wear off and I'd still be left with the deep longing for true connection, for something meaningful and lasting.

In reality, I was subconsciously keeping these men at arm's length for fear that if they got too close, they'd see just how unlovable I really was. And then my ego would crumble. But after the orgasm, the emptiness echoed even more loudly within me.

Eventually, I learned that I could forgive myself and start fresh if I was willing to change the old behaviors I was relying on to prop me up. I learned that I could defeat my shame with a steady dose of self-love. I learned that I was in the driver's seat all along but following someone else's map. It was time to throw that out the window and go on my intuition.

In hindsight, I see how the sexual abuse from my sister and the feeling of abandonment I internalized from my relationship with my mom created a perfect storm that made me desperate for love—desperate to feel desired. The alcohol was initially just a substitute for the pain, but it ended up becoming the vehicle for even more of it to enter my life. Ultimately, my conscious awareness of these underlying factors was the gateway to releasing the past and replacing it with the healing power of self-acceptance and grace.

I'm fascinated by the concept of grace. The idea that even though you've wronged yourself or others, you're still worthy of the blessing of belonging is a deeply validating thought. And a cleansing one, too. Grace whispers to me in bouts of anger, and helps me return to compassion more quickly. *We're all just doing the best we can,* it says. Grace whispers to me in moments of anguish, and helps me return to hope more easily. *Everything is a spiritual assignment,* it tells me. Grace whispers to me in times of tragedy, and reminds me that everything is going to be okay. All I have to do is surrender and trust. *You are being guided. Have faith,* it reassures me.

Grace is the voice of healing and love that bursts forth from your divinity within. When you feel like you've lost your way or like you can never start over or be forgiven, always remember that you can shed who you once were and embrace who you really are: A divinely-appointed presence with the power to consciously choose. We will revisit the concept of grace in the **Accepting** section. For now, just know that it was instrumental in helping me wipe the slate clean. Even though I felt my actions had tarnished me forever, in the eyes of a higher power they actually polished and revealed me as perfectly human exactly as I am.

Grace, forgiveness, and conscientious living represent a revolving door of a different kind: One that doesn't keep you locked in a spin cycle of shame, going 'round and 'round until you're dizzy, disoriented, and disempowered—but rather a portal that whisks you more quickly back to yourself. Just as you're about to make another unconscious choice.

THE TWO SHIPS

We had no choice but to surrender.

After dashing through a parking lot that was more like an Olympic-sized swimming pool in the middle of a torrential downpour at 6 a.m., my friend, Hunter, and I handed over our sopping-wet tickets and stepped aboard our home for the next three hours.

The Key West Express seems like a perfectly great mode of transport from Fort Myers to the Florida Keys: It's a large boat with two fully-stocked bars, several TVs, and multiple levels of seats for a smooth and comfortable ride to Florida's southernmost point.

Except when there's a hurricane in the Gulf of Mexico.

No more than a half hour into our adventure, the Key West Express encountered ten-foot swells in the gulf. The once-polite passengers quickly fell into a state of fervent frenzy I've only ever witnessed on a movie screen before. People were running for the restrooms, couples were clamoring for trashcans, and groups were grasping for barf bags. Pandemonium and puke had instantly become our new normal. It was impacting everyone on the boat. Save for the two of us.

Everything around us was in complete and utter chaos, but Hunter and I remained cool and composed. Truth be told, there was a certain comfort that emerged for me even in the midst of that calamity. My body and mind had become accustomed to the uncertainty and discomfort of the ride until it felt like business as usual—my new normal out on the open sea.

With nowhere to run and nothing to do about the effects of the hurricane, we were faced with a clear choice: Complain about the circumstances or concede to them. Considering that neither one of us could stomach what we were witnessing, we remained silent and chose to surrender instead. When Key West finally appeared on the horizon, Hunter and I looked at each other, let out a sigh of relief, and smiled. The other passengers cheered and exchanged high fives—joyous that they made it through those challenging waters. I've never seen people so happy to see land in my life.

Except for myself on one other occasion.

Three years before my trip on the Key West Express, my boyfriend at the time chartered a 35-foot boat with his best friend. We woke up before dawn and rode out 65 miles from the coast of Delaware to go deep-sea fishing for the day. Not wanting to feel left out of the fun, I accepted their invitation to tag along.

I had no idea what I signed up for. Because we departed so early, I was able to initially get by while sleeping on a bench just inside the cabin at the back of the boat. When I awoke a couple of hours later, I felt tired, nauseous, hungry, and afraid. I was handed a drumstick of fried chicken and a beer from the cooler—age-old, ice-cold coping mechanisms for those weary of the waves. But neither assuaged me; no matter what I did, I couldn't seem to calm down and accept the uncertainty of feeling so cut off from the rest of the world. There was no cell service. There was no land in sight. There were just waves and ocean as far as the eye could see. I felt stranded and alone. I was scared and bored and desperately wanted to get back to put my feet on dry land. Instead of giving in and making the most of the trip, I resisted and refused to embrace the moment. That normal day out on the Atlantic was miserable for me. And what should have been a miserable day on the Key West Express actually became normal once I got used to it. The only difference was how I showed up for the assignments laid out for me. I finally found peace when I gave up trying to change what couldn't be changed.

QUE SERÁ, SERÁ

Here's the thing about giving up control: It's not about doing nothing, it's about knowing when there's nothing you can do. If you continue to resist even when the only choice you have is to renounce, you will create rough seas where there are none.

It's not what's happening *around* you; it's what's happening *inside* you that's important. It's not where you go in life that counts; it's how you carry yourself as you get there. Your outer reality is a reflection of your inner state of being. What you try to control around you is only an attempt to provide more emotional security and a sense of safety within.

It's amazing what happens when you let go of the need to control and instead welcome each moment as it is. The ocean becomes calm, even in the midst of a hurricane. Cold fried chicken warms your soul. Paradise waits not on the other side of the storm, but deep in its depths in the fullness of your heart.

RESISTING AND PERSISTING

Whether it's to protect ourselves from feeling bad or preserve what makes us feel good, resistance is a choice, made unconsciously, to combat Change. It shows up in many forms, such as our addictive patterns, our desire to control, and our stories. When we unintentionally invest our energy this way, we buy stock in the very prison that mentally holds us captive. This is a sacrilegious choice we make against ourselves. We are ordained to be free and to exercise our willpower for our own good and the goodwill of others. When we do not act in this capacity, we undermine our growth and stumble from the path of highest good. Like a parasite of our own choosing, resistance saps us, makes us self-sabotage, causes us to over-control, and encourages us to avoid the assignments that will help us advance along our path. In the end, this does nothing except drain us of our time and energy. Anything we avoid is amplified and anything we bury is bolstered. Eckhart Tolle addressed this when he said, "Whatever you fight, you strengthen, and what you resist, persists."

Resisting is a disempowering choice that paralyzes us. We sacrifice ourselves when we refuse to surrender to things that cannot be changed. As you read in the previous chapters, I've done this. I spent precious years of my life refusing to allow reality to be as it was. I repressed the trauma I experienced with my sister. I repudiated the deaths of my mom and my grandfather. I racked up a multitude of sexual partners.

In all of my resisting, the biggest lesson I learned was in regards to my choices. One of the smartest choices you can make in life is to surrender to your spiritual assignments when they reveal themselves. Do not delay, dismiss, refuse, or resist. Your path of highest good is also your path of least resistance. It is the clearest, least complicated path for you. It is paved with exercises in acceptance. The first task is to accept the path itself. It is your life's purpose to walk it.

Resistance is a turn away from the light of consciousness and into the darkness of unconsciousness instead. We cast a shadow on anything we touch when we do it unconsciously. The entire energetic frequency of a situation is lowered when you live life this way. But I promise you this: If you shed the light of your awareness on the darkness of your resistance, it will shrink, diminish, and wither away. This transformation is yours to claim. Awareness is a form of alchemy; it will turn all your anguish into gold.

In the end, there's only one thing that we should resist: Resistance itself. When we renounce our resistance and bring it into our conscious awareness, we diffuse its power over us. We can inquire into our motives by asking empowering and emancipating questions such as: *Am I fighting the flow of life? Is this resistance productive? What would this situation look like if I just accepted it instead?* The light of awareness casts out the shadows of our stories and we enter a space of grace and glory. When held up to light, our resistance shows us what we need to heal. Once we are aware, we become aligned with the divine and supported in our growth. We are given the strength to let go and the courage to accept what we used to think was unacceptable. We are granted a miracle.

> Awareness is a form of alchemy; it will turn all your anguish into gold.

In the light of understanding, anything is possible, anything is accessible, and everything is healed. Including you, dear one.

3
Accepting

THE SHIFT

"You have 60 seconds to explain yourself," I said to my boyfriend, dropping his iPad in front of him. "I know what's been going on," I said, jolting him awake.

"What do you mean you 'know what's been going on?'" He asked, sitting up as he yawned.

"You know exactly what I mean," I said, listing the dating apps and corresponding messages I discovered when I plugged his iPad in to charge it. "I know you've been talking to other guys and exchanging photos with them. I read through everything just now."

"I don't know what to say," he said.

"Well, you can start by saying that you're sorry or that you didn't mean to hurt me or any number of other reasonably sympathetic responses," I said, thinking this should've been easier than it was shaping up to be. An uncomfortable silence sat thick in the air before he opened his mouth to speak again.

"I guess it's kind of like porn to me," he said before another long pause. "I didn't meet anyone so I don't see what the big deal is."

"We've supposedly been in a committed relationship for six

months now," I said through clenched teeth. "You shouldn't be sending x-rated pictures to random guys nearby. You might not have met anyone yet, but they're super close."

His insincerity and deflection continued for several more minutes before I excused myself to go for a calming walk around the block. I was flabbergasted. I felt like our relationship was broken. I felt betrayed. The anger and disbelief gave way to anguish and regret. *Maybe you did something to deserve this,* my inner voice said, beginning its age-old attacks. *You always mess things up.*

I pushed the self-defeating and disempowering thoughts out of my head and composed myself. As I laid down in my boyfriend's bed, reality sank in: We were flying to Vermont the next morning to meet two of my best friends for a weekend of skiing while staying at a condo owned by my boyfriend's dad. *Suck it up until after this weekend*, I thought in my sleeplessness. *You can figure it all out then.* My inner voice of reason agreed, not wanting to subject my friends to the drama. Another burden became buried in the underbelly, another pile of embers swept under the rug.

The weekend in the mountains came and went. My friends didn't seem to suspect anything. We were even able to have a little fun while there. I was convinced I had successfully pulled off my covert cover-up mission.

Eventually, winter gave way to spring, then summer, then autumn. Soon enough, my 60-second grace period turned into a six-month one. But no apology ever came. In fact, I felt like our situation continued to deteriorate over time. Each time, the cycle went predictably like so: A transgression, a breakup, a reunion, and a settlement. Each round felt like another avalanche, the mountain of our love shedding layers until all that remained was stone and dirt, until I was in a relationship that was no longer healthy with a man I no longer recognized. I had unconsciously chosen to remain in a situation that no longer served me and I felt myself suffocating under the landslide as a result.

But the Universe had bigger and better plans for me.

A few weeks after I got back to New York from that trip to the mountains, I turned another page—this time in my career. I was heading up social media for a magazine, and finally had my first employee to manage as well. His name was Ben. I'll never forget our first encounter in the basement of the massive building in Midtown where we worked. We instantly connected while waiting to get our portraits taken for our work IDs on our first day.

"This is bound to be one wild ride," said Ben, excited to be working at his first major magazine in New York.

"You got that right," I said, giving him a high-five and a nod of approval. "We better buckle up." The two of us shared our first of many laughs.

In the weeks and months that passed, Ben and I got to know one another over lunches at work and drinks after hours. We spoke about personal and professional goals. We shared the wonders of living in New York. We talked about our respective relationship challenges over the years and the growth we both experienced as a result. Ben and I became fast friends and close confidants.

My long-distance relationship crashed and burned later that same year. A few weeks after the brutal breakup, I was up late one night struggling to sleep. I was exhausted and defeated, feeling like I had hit rock bottom while I stared at the bedroom ceiling in the dark.

ACCEPTING

At around 2 a.m., I decided to turn on the light and put my two feet on the floor. I turned around to face my bed and got down on my knees. I leaned my forearms against the duvet and clasped my hands together tightly. I prayed. It was the first time in many years that I had an inner dialogue with God:

Hi, God. If you're hearing this, I could use some help right now. I'm really struggling and I don't want to carry this burden anymore. Please grant me the strength I need to let go and carry on. Please show me the way. Amen.

I opened my eyes, half expecting a guy in robes to be standing there, waiting to give me a lecture or a hug—or both. I climbed back into bed when a soft, hushed voice entered my head. *Check your email*, it said.

Unable to fall asleep, I obliged. I started scanning through old emails and came across this one I sent to my boss at the magazine a couple of weeks before I started: "Ben's awesome. He gets two thumbs up from me. What are the next steps to get him in the door and on the team?" The date on the email was March 12. *That's strange*, I thought. *I know that date from somewhere.* I checked the calendar to investigate, and it finally dawned on me: I first spoke to Ben on the same night that I discovered my boyfriend was cheating on me. I put the phone down as I cupped my mouth and cried. My prayer for strength and clarity was granted. I was shown that the Universe sent me an angel just before the first avalanche was unleashed on my relationship. Life was speaking to me in that moment, and I finally had the clarity to hear it. The synchronicity was simply impossible to ignore. Ben was a sounding board, a shoulder to cry on, a fierce friend. I needed to let go of the rotted rope that my relationship had become, and Ben was the mirror to help me realize I had the strength within me to do so.

Recognizing the importance of Ben's appearance in my life was the very definition of a miracle. This alteration in the way I was looking at the events of my life changed me forever. Once I recognized Ben for the Godsend that he was, there was no turning back.

I was experiencing what I call The Shift. The Shift occurs when something so revolutionary happens in your life that you have no choice but to reorganize your thoughts and reinterpret your experiences through this new lens. Your life becomes divided into before and after The Shift occurs. Try as you may, there's no going back to the way things were before. You have experienced an earthquake of the mind—a massive and momentous transformation of perspective that completely shakes up and changes how you approach the world. That's the power of The Shift. That's the power of prayer. That's the power of miracles.

Looking back on this situation years later and from a new vantage point, I no longer feel bruised; I feel blessed. I no longer feel hurt because I found healing. I no longer feel pain because I found perspective. Yes, I caught my significant other cheating on me. But I also made a formidable friend in Ben that same day. I don't think it gets any more poignant or poetic. That sleepless night in my room, I realized that Ben was a guiding light that parted the mists and pulled me out of the deep darkness of a toxic relationship. And the first of many miracles I now had the eyes to see.

ACCEPTING

THE GREAT TRANSLATION

Miracles occur when you are willing to clear your mind and open your heart in order to see a situation differently and through the lens of love. Suddenly, the past loses its power over us and we embrace the now. We develop distaste for the drama on which our stories used to survive. The darkness loses its allure. We trade resistance for assistance, turning over our heaviness to the heavens. We pray for guidance, courage, and peace. We're finally ready to see clearly. Reinhold Niebuhr's *Serenity Prayer* captures this sentiment well:

> *God, grant me the serenity*
> *to accept the things I cannot change,*
> *the courage to change the things I can,*
> *and the wisdom to know the difference.*
> *Living one day at a time,*
> *enjoying one moment at a time;*
> *accepting hardship as a pathway to peace;*
> *taking, as Jesus did,*
> *this sinful world as it is,*
> *not as I would have it;*
> *trusting that You will make all things right*
> *if I surrender to Your will;*
> *so that I may be reasonably happy in this life*
> *and supremely happy with You forever in the next.*
> *Amen.*

The *Serenity Prayer* is a powerful spiritual teacher. The word serenity is based on the Latin word *serenus*, which means clear. The clarity we need for miracles to occur is granted when we pray for serenity. We are gifted the wonder of true sight—the sacred ability to adjust our perspective and see things with a conscious and spiritual awareness. I experienced this sight when I decided to turn my burdens over to a higher power after my breakup. My Shift showed me how much support I was afforded in Ben, even when I failed to recognize it.

As the *Serenity Prayer* says, we need this clear vision in order to see two fundamental perspectives that govern our lives. The first perspective is to accept what cannot be changed. Acceptance is a translation. It takes everything that we've misunderstood about our past and expresses it in the language of love and redemption. We reframe our stories through acceptance. Like rain that falls on a forest engulfed in flames, acceptance douses our doubts and dismisses our despair, helping to clear the air of destruction and resuscitate our love, joy, and peace.

There are days when I look back on all the wrong turns I feel I made, and I cringe. Judgment swoops in and pulls me into its grasp yet again. But then acceptance comes in to save me and I am born again from the ashes. Acceptance writes off the debt of your past. You no longer have to answer to your pain when it knocks again. You reach a new level of awareness when you accept what's come to pass. Clarity clears the way. Letting go feels natural when you're not expending your energy to bring your burdens with you. A lightness of spirit emerges. True acceptance takes what we have unknowingly resisted in darkness to something that we knowingly accept in the light. This choice cannot be undervalued. You are choosing to bring your past to light and see it clearly. This is tremendously brave because it is incredibly painful. The more we avoided or resisted the pain of the past, the more it hurts when it comes up again.

But, like all pain, it is temporary. The closer we get to these painful memories and stories, the more we understand their true nature. Our emotional pain is quite often an act of resistance against our own love, our own depth of being, and our own power to choose. This realization can be shocking to accept.

Acceptance is the most powerful peace agreement you can make with your past, with anything that cannot be changed. This treaty absolves any wrong turns you feel that you or someone else made because there is no changing them. They were made and they brought you here, back to clarity despite all of your attempts not to see or feel.

The agreement of acceptance is binding. It admits that there is no fruit to be harvested from the rotting tree of resistance except for poisonous anti-truths. A new tree is planted in place of the old one. This tree of acceptance blossoms easily. It nurtures us with the freshness of forgiveness, the glee of gratitude, and the grandeur of grace. These are all forms of acceptance, doorways back to the path of highest good, and stepping-stones back to our highest selves. But they aren't the only way.

The other perspective that serenity grants us is the clarity to change what we can. Whether it's how we spend our time, the friends we decide to grow close with, or choosing to show up and be vulnerable, we have the ability to make powerful choices that can impact our health and well-being. I will cover this in the **Choosing** section of the book. For now, it's important to know that choosing to change those internal and external elements in our lives that keep us from our path of highest good is not just right, it's necessary. We must choose to plant new trees alongside the trees of acceptance. Eventually, with care and time, our forest will grow again from the flames that once destroyed its delicate roots. Serenity is the first step toward being restored and renewed. This clarity brings us back to the light in two ways:

1. It shows us that we must accept the things we cannot Change.
2. It reinstates our power to choose to Change the things we can.

This section will dive deep into the former. We'll explore the hidden power of radical acceptance. We'll discuss the importance of belonging to yourself above anyone else. We'll navigate what it's like to fiercely forgive those folks whom we feel have wronged us. We'll roll up our sleeves and cultivate gratitude for how the past shaped us into the people we are today. This is where the work begins. I will show you the exact tools, tips, and techniques I used to transcend the traumas I described in the **Resisting** section. I'll walk you step-by-step through the process so you can follow in my footsteps. These activities in acceptance can completely transform your life. All you have to do is allow them.

RADICAL ACCEPTANCE

No matter how hard we try, some things in life just can't be changed. When we unconsciously choose to resist, we poison our hearts and our minds. We fight and kick and scream and tug against the current of life. In the end, we have nothing to show for our resistance. Like trying to leave a footprint in the ocean, our attempts are futile and easily covered over by the tides of time.

Acceptance is the antidote to resistance. It takes our fearful stories and returns them to love. We are healed when we welcome acceptance into our lives with open arms. When we accept what has happened, we put a salve on our heart. A thought, a chapter, an era is finally finished. We can mend.

The past cannot be changed. Death cannot be reversed. The court of logic cannot convince your heart. These are essential truths of our existence. And what cannot be changed must be bravely, fearlessly, radically accepted.

Radical acceptance is a practice from a branch of psychology called Dialectical Behavioral Therapy. It is especially helpful for those who may have experienced emotional or physical trauma because it counters our natural inclination to resist or repress the pain associated with these events. As the name suggests, radical acceptance is a direct defiance of our avoidance strategies and a way to formally accept what cannot be changed.

Our patterns of resistance run deep. It takes bold resolve and absolute action to jolt us out of these grooves in the pavement. We must veer off the course of comfort and deliver ourselves to the doorstep of acceptance instead—readily and radically giving ourselves over to its healing powers. For some circumstances, this course correction is minor and will require little effort. For others, it is major and will take several attempts before it sinks in. The energy required to accept is directly proportional to the amount of energy we spent resisting. The more we cling to how we think things should be, the more effort it will take to adjust to and accept the way they actually are.

Effort and energy aside, there are some other compelling reasons to practice radical acceptance. First, it is a return to the truth. We are blinded and intoxicated by our stories. Radical acceptance helps us sober up to reality—to see with the clear vision of serenity. Second, it is the permission slip we've been waiting for. When we give up resistance and give way to acceptance, we finally give ourselves permission to let go and move forward. Lastly, it is freeing. Acceptance is the key to the chains that bind us to our pain. When we acknowledge, allow, and accept what has come to pass, we are no longer enslaved to it. Freedom is always available to those who are willing to welcome acceptance into their hearts again and again and again. This stuff takes work. It is rarely a simple one-and-done affair. So how do we actually practice radical forgiveness? We accept what cannot be changed by doing the work of accepting. Here's what you need to be willing to do:

- Go inside and dig deeper than you ever have before.
- Let go of resistance, resentment, and your stories.
- Wipe the slate clean through forgiveness and grace.
- Look for the good through gratitude.
- Rewire our brains through new experiences.

The first thing we need to do is be willing to dig deeper than we ever have before. We've spent years burying our burdens and avoiding our assignments. There are layers upon layers of stories, emotions, and beliefs piled on top of our painful experiences. You must be willing to excavate these experiences, to pull them out like weeds in a garden. Radical acceptance will require you to get utterly raw and real with yourself about your past. You have to be willing to *go there*—to brave the unexplored terrain within that you've avoided trudging through until now. This is truly the most critical part of the process because if you don't dig deep, you can't gouge out the gunk that's blocking you. Strap on your boots and grab your shovel. It's time to start digging.

The second step to fully accept reality is to let go. We become so deeply ingrained in our ways and entrenched in our stories that we are utterly attached to them. These patterns of behavior have propped us up for a long time, so there will be a considerable amount of discomfort when we let go. But in order for the new ways to take hold, we have to be willing to let the old ways die. This means no more sob stories, no more personal victimization, and no more self-pity. Resentment cannot reside in a heart that's fully accepted its past. To be clean, we must be willing to be cleansed of anything that is not pure. That includes our anger, our anguish, and our anxiety. Nothing except acceptance can stay.

The third step is how we go about that cleansing. And that's through forgiveness and grace. Forgiveness clears the air—it's a filter through which we're able to remove resentment, judgment, and negativity. This is an active choice and a surrendered process. Like the liver purges the body of toxic chemicals, forgiveness purges our minds and our hearts of anything other than love. Grace, on the other hand, is a sacred gift of worthiness and favor that's bestowed upon us by God. When you call upon a higher power, you are granted the gift of grace. You are inherently worthy of it. The heavens grace you with love when you ask for it. This love helps us remember without resentment, bringing us to the cleansing of forgiveness more easily.

The next step on the road to acceptance is to find the good all around you and within you by cultivating gratitude. Gratitude is the act of consciously saying thanks for all of the ways big and small we are blessed each and every day. When we train our minds to not just look at the negative, we're able to see the full scope of our existence and remain focused on growth. Even the most painful situation contains a seed of growth within it. All you have to do is train yourself to look for it. Gratitude is that practice.

Last but not least, the final step in acceptance is to rewire our brains through new experiences. Our minds are malleable. New chapters have the power to outshine old ones. The more we're able to explore what makes us feel happy and fulfilled, the more we tend to forget just how bad things were before. Our painful memories of the past feel much further away when we're busy creating happier ones now. This final step of acceptance helps us make a giant leap forward. It is the gateway between what has happened and what's to come. It is how we lay the past to rest once and for all. It is our power to choose. I'll delve deeper into this in the **Choosing** section. For now, understand that if you're tired of the same old story that's been playing on a loop, it may be time to record over it.

We've talked a lot about what acceptance is, but we haven't talked at all about what it isn't. One of the biggest lessons I've learned is that acceptance is not approval. You are not condoning your actions or the actions of another. In fact, what you're doing is dismissing the necessity for approval at all. Does it really matter if it was right or wrong? It happened. There is no do-over. Better to accept the situation than have it loom ominously over you forever. Blame is a game to keep you locked in shame. Refuse to play it by accepting the truth of what happened while understanding that this is not a green light for it to happen again.

Acceptance is also not apathy. You are still allowed to care. You should recognize that what happened is a part of you, not the whole you. This is about putting your heart to rest. You can't do that if you're constantly carrying the weight of the past with you. Accept what happened and find a way to productively channel your energy. When you accept, you do not bargain. True acceptance is an all-or-nothing agreement. You can accept little by little if you prefer, but you will not be granted any concessions by doing so. Remember, there's nothing to be gained by resisting what can't be changed. The sooner you can come to terms with it, the sooner you can make progress. There comes a point where we have to make a choice: *Do I want to be right or do I want to be at peace?* Some things just aren't worth fighting—most of all battles that are genuinely unwinnable.

There are some battles for which it is noble to fight that will wage on long after we are gone. Progress requires sacrifice. But this is fighting *for* Change, not *against* it. It is only when we try to change the unchangeable that we fall from grace and suffer. Surrender is the only option left in these circumstances. It is the only way to make it to tomorrow without the second arrow of suffering lodging itself in our hearts once again.

Acceptance is available at any time in any place to any person. It is a hidden treasure in plain sight. When we approach it wholeheartedly, we unlock liberation. In the end, the most important decision you will make is whether you are with the flow of life or against it. Acceptance is how we remain with the flow of life. When you answer the call and show up fully for your life regardless of the circumstances, you open the gates of heaven, you reach nirvana, and you achieve Zen. All of the great spiritual teachers reference this phenomenon. When you're with the flow of life, the flow of life is with you. It's as simple as that.

A RARE RAINBOW

It was one of the bravest things I've ever done.

The brisk November breeze was blustering against my face. The trees shook with trepidation as I waltzed into the lobby at school with an air of warmth that defied the weather. Students were gathered as usual in the main entryway waiting for the homeroom bell to ring.

Stories were being told. Homework was being finished. Minds were being molded. This time, it was my turn to take the lead. I pulled aside a handful of my best friends—a group of girls I befriended in the first three months of our freshman year of high school.

"I have something important to share," I said, commanding their undivided attention. "I'm gay, and I want you to tell everyone you talk to today so I don't have to." I ripped off the Band-Aid swiftly and succinctly, delegating the duty of having the same dubious discussion over and over. Hands went over mouths. Hugs were had. Smiles were shared.

Once the group settled down, the girls thanked me for sharing my secret and wrapped me in a bubble of love and support. "We knew it all along," they said. "Now we can finally talk about boys together!" They were encouraging and excited, and agreed to carry out the deed. They went to work straight away.

At first, the news spread directly from my delegates in one-on-one conversations with some of their close friends. From there, the story picked up steam, reaching second- and third-degree connections—people I didn't know and would never actually meet were catching wind of the news and passing it on. By the end of the day nearly every student, teacher, and administrator knew there was a gay boy in their midst, and that the gay boy was me. I walked arm-in-arm out of the building after school with one of the same girlfriends that helped me burst out of the closet. As we exited, faculty members seemed to grin a little wider, students seemed to stare a little longer, and the sun seemed to shine a little brighter than usual for a cold November day.

A rainbow was born.

BELONGING TO YOURSELF

The willingness to go out on a limb alone is one of our clearest measures of courage. In retrospect, what I did that frigid day my freshman year of high school was nothing short of remarkable. There are times, even now, when I look back and marvel at the bravery and vulnerability I was able to muster at just 14 years old. The sheer candor of my public display of acceptance inspires me and gives me hope to this day.

I am by no means the first person to come out of the closet as gay. Each and every day, people within the LGBTQ+ community own their truth by coming out of the closet. I was, however, the first gay person many of my friends and classmates ever knew—a familiar face to what would've otherwise been an unknown other. This visibility is massively important because it helps to foster acceptance. First, you must be willing to accept yourself. The bravery it took to stand on my own and claim my identity was a proclamation of acceptance not just for myself, but also for the entire LGBTQ+ community. The audacity to be utterly me was a courageous choice that took years to make. Even as a white male, choosing to come out of the closet felt daunting. *What if my friends and family don't accept me?* I thought. *Will life be more difficult if I decide to do this?* I wondered. In the end, my courage outweighed my doubts. I forged forward despite the potential drawbacks.

Revealing our truth is scary. But this is what it means to dare greatly. Despite all the odds against us—all the potential persecution and pain—we stand tall and become proud. This choice has ripple effects. Truth is freedom, for us and for those whom we decide to tell. That's the real power of coming out: It's just as much for everyone around us as it is for ourselves.

Sometimes you have to be the bird that breaks with the flock. This is scary because it makes you feel vulnerable. This exposure puts you under a spotlight and makes you a potential target for the voices to shout from the shadows. But it's also how you soar. Going deeper than you've ever ventured into the unknown can bewilder you. And yet this is where freedom and inspiration reside, where the currents lift you higher into the sky than you could ever fly before. This type of freedom is deeply contagious. As an act of pure integrity and authenticity, it inspires others to stand on their own, too.

It's extraordinary to see someone accept the light and reveal the truth within. The weariness and weight that once dominated our lives start to feel tolerable. *If they can do it I can too*, we say to ourselves. We are moved to action by people who are at peace with themselves. On some level we can sense the absence of resistance and the presence of acceptance. Acceptance is alluring. We are drawn to it like bees to nectar. When we recognize the aura of acceptance in another, we are reminded of our own ability to accept. It is a call to courage, a summoning of our spirit. Ultimately, it is our duty to decide: *Can I venture out on my own? Am I willing to stand in solidarity with myself above all else? Do I dare to let go of the darkness and embrace the light?*

This is hallowed ground—a space reserved for reverence, where we respect the gravity of the choice to stand alone out on the ledge. Bravery, it turns out, is just as much about the mundane moments as it is about those upon which it feels like the fate of everything rests. It's being grateful to be alive, having the grit to show up, and having the gumption to exist in a land outside of expectation. It is in the depths of this vastness where we see ourselves clearly, where we find ourselves again. *It's good to see you again*, whispers the wilderness. *It's good to see me again, too*, you whisper in acceptance. The trees shake as they smile.

THE FOUR LOVE LETTERS

Four love letters completely changed the trajectory of my life. The first letter arrived in the mail the week of Thanksgiving several years ago.

"You are truly special and unparalleled in this world. I love you now and always," he wrote. I put the note down and the dam broke open. The stories that said, *You'll never find anyone else* evaporated. The fearful thoughts that told me, *No one wants you* were cast out. The heaviness I felt in my heart was lifted. All that was left was the truth. And a tear-soaked yellow envelope.

It was three weeks after the end of my relationship with the ex who cheated—and the beginning of a new relationship with myself—when I received that unexpected card in the mail. It was one of only two cards I ever received from him. In this one, he opened up in a way I'd never witnessed before.

"When we first met, I told you one of the reasons I liked you is I thought you could make me a better person. And, while I didn't often say it, I feel that you've had—and will continue to have—a profound impact on my life," he said. When I needed it most, I was reminded of the incomparable power of unconditional love.

It's a miracle when someone opens up and communicates straight from the heart. It's an act of selflessness that can disarm the most rigid and deep-seated fear in any situation in which it's wielded. It's a force of light that drives out the darkness and reverts us to the path of highest possible good. Expressing love in this way is a potent and innate power that seems to have been long forgotten. Even and perhaps especially in today's era of abundant communication and connectedness, it is a rare treasure. But then a friend or a sibling or a lost love comes along and mirrors you back to you—and you get a glimpse of your spirit. You finally see that you're just a force of love that's forgotten who you really are. Even in your forgetfulness, the truth remains. Love is in your bones, sweet one. It can't be otherwise. It's everything that's been piled on top of that love that's tarnishing and suffocating your truth. You have been conditioned to believe the fear that you're not beautiful, not brilliant, not bespoke. Those are just falsehoods in which you've mistakenly placed your faith. Love is your birthright. Regardless of what you chose to believe before, this certainty remains. And so it was with me as well.

A week after I received that reminder from my ex, a second letter changed my life. This one reasserted my truth. This one reaffirmed my value. This one celebrated my strength. It was the very first love letter I ever wrote to myself.

Dear Chris,

You've had your heart broken more than anyone I know; yet you never let it break your spirit. I am humbled by how much you've been through yet how optimistic you remain. I'm amazed at how resilient yet compassionate you are. Always remember: While you may not understand how this pain can transform into something truly great, it can and it will because it's happened for you time and time again.

I love how well you know yourself and how you laugh at every chance you get. You constantly challenge yourself to do better and be better, and I admire that so much. Your work ethic makes me want to be a better man. I care for you deeply because I see how much you care about your passions and the people with whom you surround yourself. You are an inspiration to so many and I love seeing how your words can rally the masses. You are a warm, gentle soul and you deserve to be surrounded by people who appreciate and cherish that about you. Everything you've ever dreamed of will come to you if you just believe in yourself, learn what you can, have faith, and let life unfold as it's meant to.

Your beauty comes from the inside—and that's why I love you. Cheers to bigger and better things to come.

With all my heart,
Chris

Learning to love myself was like nature waking up after a long winter. The card from my ex was one of the first warm spring days, welding the pieces of my heart back together as they thawed. The heat cascaded over me, melting the icy tips that had formed, transforming my once-frozen exterior into trickling trails of truth. The dew dripped and dropped deep down into my roots, hydrating my desiccated determination—giving me the strength I needed to carry onward to a new day. Together, these forces helped me bloom in all areas of my life. A deluge of Change had arrived. That's the beautiful thing about love: It multiplies.

I was irreversibly altered when I received that yellow envelope in the mail. An awakening occurred. The light of consciousness stepped in and healed my stories once again. I was reminded that I'm treasured, that I matter, that I am loved. A new season had begun. But the changes didn't stop there. Three years later, a third letter changed my life. This was a love letter of a different sort—a final note addressed to my mom.

Dear Mom,

I'm writing you this letter to say my final goodbye.
A lot has changed in the 12 years since you passed. I've grown into a man I'm confident you'd be proud to call a son: I have a successful career, a thriving social life, and a lot of personal passions that I long to discuss with you.
But you're gone. And you're not coming back.
I've spent the last decade trying to keep your mem-

ory alive. I've shared stories of water park visits, break-up care packages, and poolside tears—some of my fondest memories with you that I'll cherish forever.

But I've run out of epic moments to share. Truth is, we just didn't get enough time together. The echoes I used to feel grow more faint each year; the details of the times we shared together have grown fuzzy and less clear. Now all that's left are our embraces like the ones in our pictures—traces of our love frozen in time and blurry pixels.

I do know one thing for certain: I'll never forget how much you adored me.

But it's time to let go. I need to release the hurt I've kept buried inside for too long; I need to release you to move on. I know you've been wanting me to do this for some time.

And I'm finally ready.

Sleep tight, my angel—I know you'll be watching over me. I'll see you in heaven.

With all my heart,
Chris

The deaths of my mom and grandfather haunted me for many years. At first, the waves of grief were like tsunamis. In survival mode, I ran from them because I was consumed by the fear that I would drown if I ever let them touch me. But running was exhausting. Over the years, when the tsunamis would return, I started swimming, learning to move with the flow when the tide came in once more. Eventually, I was able to ride the waves as they rose. I simply allowed them to wash over me and not react. I accepted their presence in my life. That's when something magnificent happened: I floated. I survived the impact and wasn't washed away in the process. I remained to take another breath, to smile another smile, to live another day. I stayed in this raft-like state for several years, unable to drift back ashore. It was only when I wrote my mom a proper goodbye that I reasserted my ability to heal. In doing so, I finally found my footing again. The waves became more like ripples, my energy of resistance no longer amplifying their magnitude. In acceptance I found the strength to let go.

In time, I also found the same strength to extinguish the flames in my heart, to end the wars that waged inside. I reflected deeply on what Michele had done and what might have caused her to behave in the way she did. Having been through a significant amount of suffering myself, I mentally placed myself in Michele's position and learned to empathize with her because of all of the struggles she endured. Looking back at it several decades later, I recognized that she was merely passing on the pain that she could not bear. I don't know if Michele was the victim of sexual abuse herself. I'm not sure if she started the chain or was just another link within it. But here's what I do know: I was one of the only constant, loving figures in her life. I believe Michele acted in the way she did because all she really knew in her life was the feeling of being pushed away. And if she could control me in the same way she had been controlled, then maybe her life wasn't so out of control after all.

The molestation, the blackmail, the drugs—all of it was how she learned to cope with the hurt. She manipulated me and projected her pain because she simply didn't know what else to do. I believe Michele learned to hurt others the way that she was hurt—up close and deep down. Michele certainly didn't come out of the womb like that. She made the same mistake made by so many before her, internalizing the events of her life, thinking they were a reflection of her character and her worth, telling herself stories about how she didn't belong and she wasn't loved. But that couldn't be further from the truth. I loved her. She was my sister. Our bond was proof that we belonged to one another. Michele was a caring sibling and a compassionate spirit who learned through conditioning that controlling and harming both herself and those around her was how to feel something and how to survive.

Throughout my life I've seen so many people go down this dark path only to realize there's more darkness on the other side. But I learned I could choose differently. Instead of darkness, I chose light. Instead of resentment, I chose forgiveness. Instead of pain, I chose peace. Instead of shame, I chose vulnerability. And I chose all of those things again in releasing the pain she inflicted. There can be no fire without oxygen. It was time to reclaim mine.

My dearest sister Michele,

I forgive you. I'm sorry it's taken me so long to release both of us from this fire that ravaged our hearts.

I know you meant me no harm. I know you were young and only perpetuating the pain that had been inflicted upon you. I know you didn't know any better.

ACCEPTING

But you did things to me that have taken me years to unpack and fully feel—and transcend as well.

When you decided to touch me inappropriately, I didn't know what a penis or a vagina was. I didn't understand the concept of sexual abuse. And I most certainly didn't understand consent.

I trusted you implicitly and loved you with the pure heart of a child—because I was one. And you were my big sister, so who was I to question your motives? I thought you'd always have my back.

You betrayed me in a deeply hurtful way. And you didn't stop there. When you found out I was gay just a few years later, you blackmailed me into doing your bidding lest you tell mom my secret. You used my own shame against me for your gain. And I let you do it because I was too young to understand that the truth will always set you free.

That's why I'm writing you this letter now. My truth is real. My feelings are real. The hurt was real. And you never apologized for inflicting that pain, but I forgive you anyway because I choose to remember what you did but I no longer wish to feel enslaved to it.

I choose to let go. I choose to be a voice for others who have shared in this same pain. I choose not to allow this to be my identity, and, consequently, put me in a cage. I choose to extinguish the flame you lit within me so many years ago.

Even though you've passed on from the physical realm, I know you can feel a weight lifted off of you.

May you rest in even deeper peace knowing that you are forgiven. And that I'm okay.

In healing and with love,
Chris

My healing happened slowly over the course of several years. Each love letter was a building block along that path, gently guiding me back to what was of the highest good for me. The first letter was a sign, waking me up to the inimitable power of the written word to help express those things that were either difficult or impossible to verbalize out loud. While the first letter was one that I received from someone else, the other three were gifts I gave myself—blessings I felt the responsibility to bestow upon myself in order to release my resistance and move forward with my life. I directed that first blessing within, going straight to the source of my suffering. This correspondence opened up a pathway for me to appreciate all of the struggles I endured and recognize them for what they truly were: Life lessons that were guiding me back to myself. This was a crucial step because it showed me that I could choose to give myself the love and affection I felt owed by everyone else. I could choose to take responsibility for my own joy. I could choose to simultaneously liberate myself and everyone else in the process.

My mom was one such recipient of that liberation. After a dozen years spent privately and publicly keeping her memory alive, it dawned on me that the best way I could honor her was by releasing her—by allowing myself to give up resisting the truth that she was no longer a part of my physical reality and that my relationship with her had evolved into a nonphysical and spiritual one instead.

Michele was the other person to receive that same liberation. In writing her a letter, I was able to call forth the courage to speak my truth while also emancipating myself from feeling burdened by it any longer.

These four love letters were stages of my transformation, phases of my cocoon. When all was said and done I was finally ready to stop running away. And come home.

YES, AND

Forgiveness is a lighthouse for those lost at sea. It stands steadfast, arms wide open to anyone willing to walk into its embrace and finally return home.

Forgiving the past is an act of unbridled humility and compassion. It is how we wash our mental and emotional wounds, cleaning out anything that could infect or harm us. This detoxification is one of the most direct pathways to peace that's available to us. It is intentional, not accidental. You do not arrive at the lighthouse without careful navigation of arduous currents, without bringing your resistance into your conscious awareness. This is about feeling what you've previously buried, avoided, and numbed—and revisiting its frame of reference. The reference point for this pain is typically a samskara, a locked-away pocket of energy that's stored in the recesses of the mind and body. Forgiveness is the direct and deliberate act of changing your relationship to this pain. It is a *yes, and* approach to your emotions. *Yes* it happened, *and* it made you stronger. *Yes* it hurt, *and* you healed. *Yes* it sucked, *and* you survived. *Yes, and* is a form of acceptance. It acknowledges the reality of what happened and helps you cross back over the great divide from the past to the present. This shift in focus can revolutionize your entire life. It teaches you to reach for something other than resentment. And actively replace it with compassion, empathy, and love.

Forgiving is not the same as forgetting. In fact, it is the opposite. Forgiveness means choosing to remember, and doing so by selecting the lens of love and dropping everything else. It's singing the same song but in the proper key. The frequency of the experience is raised up by the focus on love. Forgiveness is an act of self-love. It is the assertion that the past has no power over you unless you say so. When you love yourself more than you cling to the memory of your pain, you're finally ready to heal. In this case, loving yourself means no longer poisoning your heart with resentment. This is a correction of an encoding error in your emotional framework. The corrupt script you've been playing over and over is rewritten and replaced. The system automatically recalibrates and reboots. The Universe always course corrects back to love if you let it.

You are ultimately greater than the sum of your pain, which is how you know you have the strength within you to let go and to forgive. Not just on a cursory level where you just go through the motions, but on a spiritual level where you feel cleansed from the burden you've carried. In theory, it should be simple to let go of your painful past because it's the most logical thing to do. But your unconscious mind is crafty and cunning—and also illogical. It will try to trick you into believing that something or someone might not need or deserve forgiveness. *What they did was unforgivable and worthy of resentment*, it asserts. *You can't let them off that easy.* But that's just it: Forgiveness is counterintuitive. You're actually letting *yourself* off the hook, not the person who hurt you. It has nothing to do with them. You haven't truly forgiven someone until you've done it to release yourself from his or her grasp.

Forgiveness is a parting of the clouds—a glimpse of the sun beaming down upon you after a season of so many storms. Weathered as you may be, your heart carries on—formidable and strong, yet fragile and soft, bending but never breaking as you're pushed and pulled through the tides of life. The burdens you bear are drops in the ocean pushing you further and further from shore until your feet can't touch the ocean floor anymore. The current pulls you in for a caged embrace. Try as you may, you can't escape its grasp. You're in the deep now and there's no turning back. There is only surrender—belly up on the open sea, drifting through your pain but never being lured down into its dark depths. You can't find your light down there. You can't make your way back to land down there. This is how you drown in your mind.

I wasn't truly able to let go of the past until I started seeing forgiveness as the life raft I needed to get back to shore, back to the lighthouse that called out to me through the shadowy mists. I suppose I always expected an apology or wanted someone else to do the heavy lifting for me. But neither of those things ever came to fruition and I was left to suffer on my own. After a while, I wasn't willing to give up the ghosts that haunted me all those years because they became familiar friends. In the end, forgiveness is both a verb and a noun. *Yes* it is something you do, *and* it is something you receive. You welcome a shift in perception and you are granted a miracle. You actively choose it and cultivate it and then surrender your judgment to be healed. You have to want peace more than you want pain, then hand over your pain as payment for that peace. *Yes* you got knocked down, *and* here you are still standing. *Yes* it was a mess, *and* you still mended.

When the lighthouse summons you through your storms, how will you answer? I know how I will: With a resounding *Yes, and.*

THE ART OF LETTING GO

There are two exercises that have rescued me and pulled me through to the dry land of acceptance. They are both vivid visualization techniques that require nothing more than a few minutes of your time and a quiet place to reflect. They each serve the same purpose: Help you release the blockages within and remember without resentment. These practices will actively utilize your mind's eye to call forth the energy from painful experiences in your past.

The first practice is a root-pulling visualization. Before you begin, make sure you scope out a quiet place where you can sit comfortably. This could be a room in your house, a patch of grass in your yard, or in a private space with friends. The key is to be able to safely and securely channel these energies without interruption. You may sit on the ground, on a pillow, or in a chair. Just make sure you are comfortable and able to concentrate. Then, follow these steps:

ACCEPTING

- Inhale and exhale deeply for five seconds each. Do this 10 times. Keep breathing deeply throughout the remainder of the exercise.
- Imagine a bright room bathed in light in your mind.
- Within that room, visualize two chairs seated across from one another. Sit down in one of the chairs.
- Call forth the person you feel wronged you—and to whom you feel connected. Picture the person seated across from you in this bright room.
- In your mind, imagine a set of roots clasped tightly around your heart, extending from your body to theirs—a symbol of the energy transfer that still connects you.
- Switch up your breathing by adding a five-second period of holding your breath between inhaling and exhaling. This is called the box breathing technique. Breathe in for five seconds, hold it for five seconds, and then breathe out for five seconds.
- Focus intently on the pain and suffering you endured because of this person. Place all your attention on it. Actively recall how hurt you were and how heavy and burdensome it felt. Sit with the discomfort.
- While holding your breath, imagine yourself pulling out the roots around your heart. Picture them falling to the floor. Feel the lightness now that they're gone. Exhale forcefully for five full seconds. Be intentional about releasing the negative energy.

Don't be surprised if you start to cry or tremble. You're allowing deep emotions to surface. You're actively releasing pent-up energies and sitting face to face in your mind with a person who hurt you. You're bound to get emotional when you feel things that you've suppressed. Repeat this process as many times as you find helpful to you. I've practiced this root-pulling visualization several times until I felt like I let go of all the negative energy from a given situation. And then I did it some more!

The second forgiveness practice builds upon the first. This exercise is an ancient Hawaiian custom for reconciliation called ho'oponopono, which translates to English as "correction." In this tradition, both parties are able to own up to their mistakes and ask for atonement in the situation. Everyone who played a part repents for their missteps and recognizes the shared hurt inflicted. The restorative practice of ho'oponopono follows four simple steps:

1. I'm sorry.
2. Please forgive me.
3. Thank you.
4. I love you.

We will follow these steps in that order as we build upon our previous root-pulling visualization. In a similar fashion, make sure you find a place where you can be calm and concentrate. Start by closing your eyes and focusing on your breath. Build up to the same box breathing technique we used before: Breathe in for five seconds, hold your breath for five seconds, and breathe out for five seconds.

ACCEPTING

Conjure the same bright room in your mind and picture two seats across from one another. When you're ready, follow these steps:

- See the person seated across from you in a room bathed in light. Look them in the eyes.
- Picture them progressing through the four steps of ho'oponopono. You remain silent while they speak.
- Imagine receiving a heartfelt apology. Internalize the feeling of receiving this closure.
- Visualize this person genuinely and sincerely asking for your forgiveness.
- Hear this person thank you for the learning opportunity, expounding upon how much it's helped them grow.
- Imagine them telling you they love you and that they didn't intend to hurt you, saying that they would've felt the same way you did if they were in your position.
- Breathe out and release the negative energy pent up between you.
- Continue breathing deeply and open your eyes when you are ready.

This visualization helps you fill in your mental gaps and try to see things from their perspective. It helps shine a light on your shared humanity and cultivates empathy between you. You're no longer predator and prey, you're two people finding common ground. In that shared space, it might also be helpful for you to walk through the same four steps in order to complete the custom. Ho'oponopono is a clear and concise way to forgive and be forgiven. It creates a space where both parties can communicate how they feel—even if that communication is hypothetical and visualized in your mind.

Whether by pulling out emotional roots or following the four principles of ho'oponopono, using your mind's eye to visualize interactions with people we feel have wronged us is a largely underutilized and highly effective tool to ground unresolved energies pent up in your unconscious mind. These techniques can be employed anywhere and at any time. All you have to do is find a place where you can be still and turn inward.

The root-pulling visualization and ho'oponopono are nimble in another way: They don't require anyone else's participation. That apology you never got? No sweat. Is the other person no longer alive? No worries. You can still give yourself the gift of forgiveness with these two practices. In fact, these are the same two tools I used to forgive my mom and my sister after each of them died. I went through these same steps over a dozen times to help me dig up and diffuse the agony within that I'd buried on their behalf.

But there's one final reason why these potent practices healed me: They helped me become open to forgiving myself. I sat across from myself in my own mind and pulled out the emotional roots. I apologized, asked for forgiveness, thanked myself, and sent my own love within. And while these two practices didn't fully cleanse the rancor I refused to fully release, they loosened my grip and exposed the cracks in my defense. I was finally ready to come to terms with the past.

ACCEPTING

THE THREE TREATIES

There are three binding treaties I've made with my past. The first is that the past has no power in the present unless I give over *my own power to choose*. The second is that I am better not just despite the past but *because of it*. The third is that the past does not matter because I am worthy of the unmerited favor of a higher power *right now*. These are more commonly known as forgiveness, gratitude, and grace, respectively, and I've committed all I have to them in my effort to radically accept the past.

Forgiveness is a fundamental act of acceptance. It wipes your energetic and emotional slate clean. And yes, you're going to think it's hard as hell. Part of why you may feel that way is because you just don't want to let go of the past. Letting go means that you don't get to be mad anymore. It means that people won't feel sorry for you and you won't get the attention and emotional pity you once received. Worst of all, you may think that forgiving invalidates the past. The reality is that forgiveness cannot change what happened. Nothing can do that. But it does release you from its grasp, it does grant you the freedom you desire. And your emotional freedom is far too important to lease out to anyone or anything else. The root-pulling visualization technique shows us how to grant ourselves this freedom. When layered with ho'oponopono, we can effectively discard our grudges, clear our blockages, and banish our bitterness. Forgiveness helps us walk through fire, sail through storms, and come back home to compassion and love.

Gratitude is another vital tool in our acceptance toolkit. Being grateful is like kintsugi for the heart; it is the gold that pieces us back together when we fall apart. No matter what happens, we are made whole again when we are able to take what we used to think of as our broken pieces, see them clearly in the light, and come to the realization that we were never really broken at all. Gratitude is a counterintuitive transmutation. It takes that which feels like a burden and turns it into a blessing. There's a little piece of heaven inside of every hell, and gratitude helps us look through the lens of serenity to see it. Like its relative forgiveness, gratitude is a selective remembering. The past is run through a strainer and the nectar of love is extracted. The practice of gratitude is replenishing in this way.

I start and finish almost every day with some sort of moment of gratitude. Sometimes, I do this mentally by stopping to appreciate something in the moment. When I'm feeling more structured, I write in a gratitude journal. All it takes is a couple of seconds to tap into this frequency of joy. Either way, the key is to make appreciation a regular practice in your life. Do it in a way that makes the most sense for you.

Grace is a cousin of gratitude, but it's distinct in its own ways. Grace is a sacrament we accept when we believe in a greater force, a higher power, an almighty God. The fabric of our Universe is imbued with this force, with this love. When we open our hearts to it, we become shrouded in that fabric, encapsulated in this energy, blanketed in its love. Grace is a gift given to those who believe in it. There is nothing else you need to do. Regardless of what you've done or what you've been through, you are made new through grace. The path of highest good is grounded in grace. Our sins are forgiven through it. Grace is the spiritual fresh coat of paint. When you accept grace, it automatically covers over that which is dirty, heavy, and painful. The darkness cannot touch you in this light. Grace is a miracle that corrects your unconscious behaviors through conscious acceptance of the highest order. There is nothing truer or more pure than grace.

I discovered this for myself on my own healing journey. Grace showed me that if God could forgive me, then so could I. This was the permission I felt I needed to let go of the resentment I had for myself after so many years spent choosing the darkness of suffering. When you are in communion with the Highest Holy, everything that's unholy falls away. While forgiveness and gratitude are gifts you give yourself, grace is a detoxification of a different kind, one that is granted to you and accepted from the Source of all things. Our stories are unraveled and a web of a different kind is woven. A fine, fresh layer of silk is placed on top in its place. It is made of pure light. It cannot be tarnished. It is indestructible.

Acceptance, as we've seen, is an unbreakable vow with the past. When we radically embrace that which we do not have the power to erase, we become pure and divine again. The path of highest good is only ever a step away. Acceptance is the step back to this path. The first task in the process of accepting the past is to go deeper inside than you've ever gone before. We do this by looking at our lives through the lens of clarity and serenity. When we do this, we see that we really only have two choices. The first choice is to come to terms with and accept that which cannot be changed. We've used our time together in this section to explore what this means. The second choice is to choose to change what we can, using our power of conscious choice to select internal and external elements that support our highest virtues, values, and vicissitudes. We will explore this concept as we progress into the next section on **Choosing**, though they are invariably intertwined.

Standing on the edge of acceptance can feel lonely and isolating. But when you are courageous enough to be in your own corner first, you will attract your tribe. This is a rite of passage we are all called to complete. In order to practice true acceptance, we must first belong to ourselves before we belong to anyone else.

The next steps in the process of acceptance involve several acts of purification and detoxification. For me, one of those acts was the lost art of writing love letters. Getting my thoughts and feelings down helped me express what I suppressed for many years.

Forgiveness, gratitude, and grace are all additional ways to exorcise our demons, extract the learning lessons, and embrace our worthiness. Together, these steps help us acquire the peace we desire. That's why we make our agreements with the past, after all, isn't it? We want peace. We are tired of chaos and calamity. Resistance costs us everything. We are spent.

There is one final way to forge a treaty with the past. In fact, it is also a treaty with the future. It is the bridge between acceptance and ascension. It is our willingness to try, our craving for new beginnings, our determination to start all over again. It is our ability to consciously and valiantly choose.

4
Choosing

WHO WILL YOU BECOME?

I was six years old when I made my first conscious choice.

I ripped open my backpack, shimmied free a flyer I picked up at school, and stormed into the kitchen.

"I don't want to play baseball, Dad; I want to play soccer!" I said, sliding the pamphlet across the mahogany table and crossing my arms. He picked it up, read it over, and placed it calmly back down. He paused for a second as a sly smirk flashed across his face.

"Alright, Son. If it's what you really want and you think it'll make you happy, I support it," he said. "But you have to finish out the baseball season."

Sports represented more than just a ball and a whistle to my dad. They were grounds upon which to prove your integrity, a field upon which to form bonds and build camaraderie, and a formidable way to formulate healthy habits. As a single parent and someone who grew up playing baseball, basketball, and hockey, he wanted nothing more than to raise a star athlete in one of those sports—a living symbol of classic Americana brought to life. I don't think he ever envisioned raising a son who would play soccer, a game he had barely heard of and knew nothing about. Of all the sports to select it was potentially the most surprising.

I was captivated by the idea that I could do something different, something that was fresh and new and exciting. So I made a choice. I took all of the energy I was putting into baseball and invested it into soccer instead. Soon enough, I retired my glove; my baseball stint faded into the background. Soccer became my world.

Over time, this decision paid dividends. I grew close to several of the players on my soccer teams and we became friends both on and off the field. Even though I had two sisters, I wasn't raised with either of them so these bonds of friendship helped me develop and grow in new and profound ways—to discover what it was like to be accountable to others and to empathize with them, too. I was committed to the teams on which I played and to the game of soccer as a whole. I learned what it meant to be invested in something bigger than myself, not just hoping but striving for the best possible outcome in each game and with every season. I was shown firsthand that hard work and determination can garner amazing results. I cultivated courage, grew my grit, and developed the desire to win.

The beautiful game kept me out of anything ugly. I invested most of my free time into soccer, which meant that I had no time to invest in anything that could've been potentially detrimental for my future. My dad understood how important it was to foster integrity, build camaraderie, and form healthy habits through sports—and soccer certainly delivered.

But none of that would've ever come to fruition if I hadn't marched home at six years old and dictated to my dad that I wanted to play soccer in the first place. From a very young age, I've had an insatiable curiosity for life and an uncanny understanding of my ability to choose for myself. Remembering this power is what has guided me through the darkness time and time again.

Carl Jung once said, "I am not what has happened to me. I am what I choose to become." At any given moment we have a choice: *Will I become what's happened, or will I become what I choose instead?* This is a critical crossroads. It is in this moment where we make a decision about who we are and what we believe our identity to be. We can go backwards or forwards. We can focus on the past or we can build a future. But you can't do both simultaneously. Either way we have the free will to choose. That's what life is really about, isn't it? The choices we make, the actions we take, the chains we break. This is how we curate and define our reality. Our ability to shape our circumstances is one of our most sacred duties.

The *Serenity Prayer* reminds us that we can either choose to accept what can't be changed or find the courage to change what we can. This is our fundamental calling in life. When we gallantly and graciously decide to build a life beyond the limitations of our past, we are granted the fortitude to do it. When we bring our awareness to the here and now we are able to shed the constraints of the past and accept our ability to create our future right this very moment.

I've made what felt like quite a few wrong turns over the years. But I've always found my way back by remembering that I have the power to choose to turn toward the light—back to what I know to be good and right and true. My intuition whispers to me in the soft seconds sandwiched between the past and the future, and asks me one vital question: *Who will you become at this moment? Me,* I answer. *Unequivocally, undeniably, unconditionally me.*

CHOOSING

THE TWO CENTERS OF GRAVITY

As early as six years old, I understood the potential we possess to mold our world and reconfigure our lives. It is our divine right to do so. We have been granted the auspicious ability to craft and create our reality. This is the single most important thing that we'll ever do.

Our lives are defined by the decisions we make. And in any given situation or circumstance, we can always choose again—we can always redefine ourselves by making a different choice. If we've fallen into judgment, we can choose compassion over sharpness. When we find ourselves lamenting, abhorring, or resenting, we can cultivate kindness and empathy instead. In those moments where fear grasps our heart in its hands, we can reach inside with a gentle, loving touch and think: *Thank you for trying to protect me but I am safe here.*

Our best choices are the ones we make with attention and intention. When we are aware of the decisions we're making and act with intention and purpose, we are supported by the highest good. Nothing can stand in our way. No obstacle is too big. No canyon is too deep. No dream is too grand. Conscious awareness is a subdued sunrise after the torment of a treacherous night. You awaken slowly but surely to the lay of the land. Everything comes into focus again.

The right answers always start with the right questions. If you want to make better choices, you have to take an honest inventory of your life. That will require self-exploration and self-reflection. This process will ask more of you than you may be used to giving. Grant yourself the permission to focus on yourself for a while. Take time and space away from others to get still and get clear about your motivations. Allow yourself to question your choices in an inquisitive and nonjudgmental manner. This is about getting to the root of why you act one way and not another—or what to do when you come to a time-honored fork in the road. You will need to get up close and personal with yourself to do this. It is when we put these areas of our lives under a microscope that we can see more clearly.

When we are willing to explore this uncharted territory—when we are willing to venture into the unknown—we start to understand what spurs our choices and what our actions are trying to tell us about ourselves. This knowledge is powerful. It gives us the data we need to take informed and enlightened action.

There's an infinite number of choices we can make, but there's a finite number of areas in our lives in which we can make them. We really only have the power to change two things: Our inner world and our outer orbit. At any given moment, we are choosing to wield our power over one or both of these two areas. Everything is a combination of these two centers of gravity.

Our inner world is ultimately all about how we pay attention. We have the means to cultivate peace by challenging our negative thoughts and selecting those that lift us instead of limit us. We're able to identify our purpose and take steps toward living within it. We can accept our spiritual assignments, follow the signs from the Universe, and live life openly, curiously, and unapologetically. The way we look at the world has a disproportionate and direct impact on the way we show up for it. When choosing to change your life, it's vital to start with the internal lens through which we view our external environment. I will divulge the steps by which we do this, helping to unbundle some of our stories and unconscious beliefs, as well as identifying how I discovered the gifts I was meant to share. Our outer orbit, on the other hand, is all about our intention. What matters to us? Why is that so? How do we live our best lives? When it comes to our environment, we possess the power to choose what we allow to influence us. We can't control what happens around us. But we *can* choose those things with which we associate—we can consciously and carefully select what we allow into our orbit to begin with. I'll walk you through how I did this with my friends and my romantic partners as well, learning to be discriminating with my time and scrutinizing the external forces I allow to sway me.

These two centers of gravity tell us what our real priorities are. Our fulfillment is a culmination of the investments we're making and the choices we're choosing. When our day-to-day life is governed by conscious choices that are backed by attention and intention, we step fully into our potential. When our inner world and outer orbit are in alignment, life feels harmonious.

A center of gravity is an inflection and reflection point. You advance or stumble, progress or regress, rise or fall in life. But only in these two areas. When we stumble, regress, and fall, we always have the opportunity to revisit a center of gravity—to select what best supports our growth in our inner world or outer orbit. Of course, these decisions feel a lot more difficult to make than they actually are. Don't be afraid to do what needs to be done to create a life that's peaceful, joyful, and uplifting for you. This is not about getting rid of the things that make you uncomfortable so you live a more comfortable existence. It is about embracing the discomfort so it feels less uncomfortable in the first place. And that will require realigning your inner and outer worlds.

When we're intentional and purposeful with what's happening inside and around us, tremendous transformation is possible. Paradoxically, when we get close to these centers of gravity, we aren't weighed down. We don't get sucked into their mass or meaning. Life feels effortless for those who know where to place their effort to begin with. Anything else is a waste of time and energy.

THE UNLIMITED MIND

It was 3 a.m. when my mind waged war on itself.

Desperate to end my racing thoughts, I reached for my phone on the nightstand. I checked up on the guy I was dating at the time. *Was he tagged in any new photos?* I wondered. *Did anyone comment or write on his profile?* I pondered. A half hour later, I set my phone down. This time, the taste of saline tears tantalized my tongue as the fear settled deep into my spine. I could feel my mind spiraling down a rabbit hole but felt helpless to halt it.

I tried scanning my body through mindfulness. I tried the box breathing technique. I tried placing my hand on my heart and sending healing energy toward the area of tightness. But the negative thoughts just wouldn't stop.

Another hour came and went while I remained in an emotional freefall. At my wits' end, I decided to get up and write. Around 4:30 a.m. my pen hit the paper.

"I'm feeling especially triggered right now," I wrote in my journal. "I feel vulnerable and exposed and anxious. My mind can't stop racing and I can't sleep, so I'm going to write until I feel like I've emptied myself of this poison." 10 pages later, I emerged lighter, calmer, and freer; a sense of peace began to settle back in. Although I never made it back to sleep, I was able to find a coping mechanism to calm me down.

My negative thoughts swoop in when I least expect it and take over my mind. They make me feel overwhelmed, inundated, and inadequate. Like an ingénue in a horror flick trying to escape her impending attacker, only to run upstairs to her certain doom—my thoughts corner me and I can't seem to break free no matter how hard or what I try.

But life doesn't have to be this way. You can liberate your mind. You can think different thoughts. You can conquer your fear and anxiety. And I'm here to show you how.

"The rational mind is really about training your brain to help you rather than hurt you," said psychiatrist Dr. Daniel Amen, while speaking about automatic negative thoughts on Jay Shetty's *On Purpose* podcast. "So often people are just brutalized by the thoughts that go through their heads… [but] you don't have to believe every stupid thing you think." In the episode, Dr. Amen went on to share his tried-and-true method for addressing these thoughts head-on.

1. Write down what you're thinking.

2. While reflecting on what you wrote, ask yourself: *Is that true?*

3. Follow up by inquiring: *Is that absolutely true?*

4. Then, pose this question in your mind: *How do I feel when I believe this thought?*

5. Next, answer this question: *Who would I be without this thought?*

6. Finally, ask this: *What's the opposite of this thought?* You might be surprised to find that the opposite of the thought that was tormenting you is usually true.

Here's an example based on the story at the outset of this chapter where I felt besieged by negative thoughts about a guy I admired. A distilled version of my writing went something like this:

1. I sent him a text earlier this morning and haven't heard back from him all day. Why would he do that? He must've found someone new. Maybe he doesn't like me after all. I should check his social media to see what he's been up to.

2. It could be true, but it's only one of many potential explanations for why he didn't respond.

3. There's actually not much objective evidence to support my subjective theories and conclusions.

4. I feel out of control and unsure of what to do when I'm uncertain of where I stand with someone. I hate that feeling.

5. Without these thoughts, I would feel safe, secure, and at peace.

6. I am worthy and well-liked with or without this guy's approval. Maybe he's feeling just as intensely about me and isn't sure how to handle it. Best to take some time and let things play out. If I continue to feel this way, I should communicate my feelings and let him know how his actions are coming across.

Here's another example. Let's say you're feeling overwhelmed with anxiety over a big career choice you're about to make. You've just received an offer for a new job and you're unsure about whether or not to accept it. Here's what the steps might look like for you:

1. This new job offer I received isn't quite what I was expecting. Is it really worth leaving where I am right now to pursue this? What if I don't like it? All of this feels so overwhelming! How am I supposed to know what to do?

2. If I calmed down I could probably figure this out.

3. I know what I'm looking for, so I guess I need to ask for that.

4. I feel out of control and unsure of what to do when I'm overwhelmed. I don't like feeling that way.

5. Instead of just feeling overwhelmed, I can focus on finding a solution that works for me.

6. I guess I'm not overwhelmed at all. I'm actually underwhelmed by the offer and need to negotiate on my own behalf.

No matter the subject or focus of your automatic negative thoughts, this line of questioning is an empowering way to reframe them. Use it in your romantic life, with your family, or even for matters concerning your career. Follow the six steps each time and you just might find that you'll feel the same sense of relief I did when I sat down to write on that sleepless night. The poison within can be used to create the antidote instead.

Another way you can unlock the unlimited potential of your mind is to challenge and rewrite your limiting beliefs. Use the following exercise to bring these thoughts out in the open and into your conscious awareness. Start by writing down some of your stories. These typically begin with phrases like, "*I never* _____," "*I can't* _____," "*I won't* _____," "*I'm too* _____," or "*I suck at* _____." Here are some of mine from previous versions of the same activity:

- I'm too clingy.
- I suck at working out.
- I hate when people waste my time.

Next, write down how these stories may have protected you in the past. When we recognize the role that our stories have played in keeping us safe, we can honor and release them. Here's what I think these same beliefs aimed to accomplish on my behalf:

- Thinking I'm "clingy" or "needy," I sabotage myself by subverting my needs. When I do this, it brings about a suffering I know how to cope with.

- Not knowing a lot about fitness is an excuse that holds me back from pursuing my goals.
- Assuming that someone intentionally wasted my time allows me to be right and to play the victim.

Finally, rewrite your limiting beliefs into affirming stories. Here's how I tracked mine through:

- I have a deep desire for intimacy and a need for closeness in my relationships—and that's perfectly acceptable. The right person for me will value this quality.
- I don't know a lot about fitness, but I'm willing to learn.
- I get to choose how I spend my time. If I feel like it's not being spent effectively, I can change my investment.

See the drastic difference in tone between the initial list of negative beliefs and the final set of rewritten stories? Reframing your inner narratives in this way will help you recognize how irrational they are, the value they played in their attempts to protect you, and how good it feels to alter them in an affirming way. This three-pronged approach from anguish to affirmation can be used for any inner narrative that might be plaguing you. Simply follow the prompts until you arrive at an end result that strips the negative lingo from your self-talk.

Whether it's through Dr. Amen's six-step line of questioning or the exercise to rewrite our limiting beliefs, these two tools can help you unlock the potential of your unlimited mind. The brain is malleable. When we reflect on and challenge our thoughts, we're able to pick and choose what we believe. Even when it feels like we can't.

THE POWER OF PURPOSE

"Don't just say it; make me *feel* it," I wrote on the white board during a college yearbook staff meeting.

It was the mantra that defined a school year—and one that's come to define my entire life.

"30 years from now, the names of the folks our fellow students are currently fawning over will become fuzzy," I said to my team. "The details of the classes they took will grow cloudy and unclear. The nights out on the town will blend together in a beautiful blur. All that will remain is how they felt about what it was like to go to school here. The rest will surely be forgotten." Their nods of approval told me they understood the emotional mandate.

This mantra and energy spilled over into everything we did that year. We photographed students in a candid, natural, and dynamic way, capturing friendships and relationships in a single shot. We designed with bright colors, bold angles, and boisterous ideas that we hadn't seen combined in yearbook form before. We painted hands and feet, legs and arms, in an effort to humanize and contextualize our high-minded ideals. It was always about how it felt for us and for the reader. If it didn't feel right, we scrapped it. As Editor in Chief, if my intuition told me that something was off, the content wasn't finalized until it had that *je ne sais quoi* feeling to it. Attending the University of Miami was an experience full of vitality and I wanted it captured and crystallized in its purest form.

The book went on to win prestigious awards and top honors from Columbia Scholastic Press Association and Associated Collegiate Press, but it was the feedback from students that rolled in when the book was finally distributed that most touched me. Random people I'd never met before messaged me on Facebook to tell me how awesome and empowering they felt the book was. Others remarked at how accurately it documented the student experience. But the greatest comments of all were the ones that recognized and marveled at how it made them feel like they were right back on campus. Upon hearing these comments, I was certain that we accomplished what we set out to do, and exceptionally grateful for the opportunity to serve as a storyteller—a conduit for memories captured in colorful pixels on glossy paper.

Growing up, I never considered myself a creative person. I used to write poetry and sing songs in my room, but those inclinations came naturally to me. I didn't realize they were actual skills that could be sharpened—talents that could be honed for professional use. It wasn't until I took an Introduction to Graphic Design class fall semester of my sophomore year of college that it dawned on me there could be something more there.

"You have the best eye for typography I've seen all semester," my professor said. *Wow. Maybe I am creative*, I thought.

Around the same time, a friend of mine who lived down the hall in my dorm and worked on the yearbook invited me to apply for an open position. After a brief but nerve-racking interview, I landed the job. Soon I discovered that the same professor that complimented me on my typography skills was also the faculty adviser of the yearbook. A little over a year later, I was interviewing for a different role, for the top editor position. I remember sitting across from that same professor and adviser, and pitching him on why I should be the Editor in Chief of the yearbook for the following school year. After I finished making my case, he simply said, "You're very green, Chris. You're either going to crash and burn or leap and soar." I assured him it would be the latter. His colleagues all agreed with me, and quickly granted the approval for me to take the role.

I'm proudly nostalgic of that era in my life. It taught me how important it is to do something with your life that makes you feel unfailingly fulfilled. I knew unshakably in my core that I had chosen well. There was no other path for me. I felt it in my bones.

I felt the same way the day I moved to New York City to pursue a career in magazines. The energy was palpable that sweltering summer evening. My feet hit the pavement with the same speed as the sweat dripping from my brow. I was eager to explore.

I sensed a pure potential in the undercurrent of the city—a stream of electricity that seemed to connect all things and all people. I realized I could meet anyone I wanted. Any contact was in reach. I could be and do anything I had the clarity to see. *Conceive it, believe it, and you can achieve it*, I thought.

On that first night in the city, I walked alone into a bar on 55th Street. Half an hour later, I met four people who worked in media. They introduced me to some of their friends, who then made introductions to another group. Before I knew it, I was home with a stack of business cards and an even bigger stockpile of hope. Six months, over 100 job applications, and countless attempts at networking later, I landed my first major gig as a social media strategist at an ad agency. A year after that, a magazine recruiter called and I leapt at the opportunity. It took over 500 days and a lot of faith, but I made my dream come true.

Telling stories has always been part of my identity, even if I wasn't always consciously aware of it. Through a series of choices made by a multitude of people, I was shown that when you act with impetus and intention all is revealed to you. My purpose revealed itself to me in this manner. I was encouraged to be creative, I was given the autonomy to explore my perspective, and I was granted the opportunity to sharpen my skills. What started as a compliment in class led to a fruitful career spent reaching billions of people online. Small steps and quiet choices led me further along my path and paved the way for breakthroughs to occur.

What have you been curious about throughout your life? What about recently? Get clear about whatever sparks joy in you and also why you think that's so. There's likely a reason for your interest in that particular area. This is how we get clarity and vision about our purpose. You explore all of those topics and talents and then try them out to see how they feel. It could be as innocent as a nifty skill turned into a hobby or as serious as a talent you'd like to pursue as a potential career. Either way, it's worth exploring your curiosity to see what makes you feel fulfilled and at home with yourself.

Maya Angelou once said, "People will forget what you said, people will forget what you did, but people will never forget how you made them feel." My soul knows that to be true. I feel it as I'm typing these words. And I hope you feel it, too. I've spent a lifetime trying not to just say something but to have others *feel it*. It's what

I'll do until I take my last breath. It is my gift, and I intend to share it with a little bit of grit, a little bit of gratitude, and a little bit of grace. For as many seconds as I'm granted.

THE VALIDATION DETOX

"I just can't do this anymore," I said, holding back tears. "Something's got to give."

I was sitting on the couch in my downtown Manhattan apartment, venting to my roommate, Courtney, when I confessed I needed to make a major life change.

"It's time to focus back on me," my 25-year-old self said, voice trembling ever so slightly. "I think I need some space so I can regroup. I'm exhausted."

"This is the best idea you've had in a long time," Courtney said, choking up as she continued. "I'm so proud of you, Chris. You know I'm here for you if you need anything."

Courtney watched as I deleted the myriad dating apps that had drained me to my core and yet somehow sustained me. An instant wave of relief washed over me and was replaced with a renewed sense of purpose. Days later, I posted an announcement:

> There are certain points in life where you have to tune out all of the distractions and say to yourself, "I need to do me." I've officially reached that point. After three years and hundreds of dates in the city, I

am emotionally exhausted and romantically drained. In the interest of self-preservation, I've decided to take a break from the NYC dating scene for a while. It's time to refocus my attention and energy on my friends, my career, and most importantly myself. So for the first six months of 2013, I will attempt a pretty difficult feat: NO dates and NO hookups—at all. (Insert gasps, laughter, and looks of confusion here.) I strongly believe this will help me finally release my emotional baggage and wipe my slate clean, so to speak. I know some of you may not understand this decision. All I ask is that you support me in my struggles and help me stay true to myself—even if it's just a simple text, "like," or comment. Lord knows I'll need it. Here we go!

My happiness and sense of belonging were built on top of a foundation of external validation. Constant stimulation was the brick and mortar that held up the House of Chris. The more packed my schedule became, the more important I felt. It was thrilling. And it was exhausting. I was young and I thought I should soak up every experience available to me.

The search for fulfillment through external validation is a paradoxical one. At first, it feels like what you should be doing: It's fun, exhilarating, and pleasurable. In the short term, you're propped up by compliments and liquid courage—and your own sense of invincibility. But the music eventually stops playing and the drinks eventually stop flowing and you go home to look at yourself in the mirror and you still have the same void; the emptiness remains because you can't find self-fulfillment from anything or anyone outside of you.

I think in some sense we all go on this journey. Not realizing that we have a wealth of beauty and belonging within us, we turn outward in search of validation, approval, and security. But we end up feeling emptier than when we started because our true value and self-worth must come from within.

Once you validate yourself, you finally find your way back to the truth: You are inherently worthy and always were. Until then, your soul always yearns for sustenance. Mine yearned for stillness instead of nights out on the town. It yearned for self-reflection and growth instead of always focusing on pleasing others. It yearned for true connection instead of hollow hook-ups. In a lot of aspects of my life, I felt like the rubber just wasn't hitting the road. It was time for a tune-up.

As I embarked on my journey, I had a short list of priorities I knew would help me accomplish my lofty goal. First, I knew that in order to be successful, I needed to re-establish personal boundaries; I knew it would be important to be able to say no. So I decided to reserve at least two nights a week for myself—and to give myself permission to turn down any function that interfered with that personal allowance. This meant saying no to birthday parties, get-togethers, and other events so I could preserve my energy and focus on my well-being. It didn't matter what the week had in store, I would always have my two nights to reflect and recharge.

Second, I knew that in order for this process to work I needed some productive activities that would enrich my life. This meant taking some of my self-prescribed "me time" to read self-help books.

It also meant using some of my time to reconnect with friends old and new. Instead of spreading myself too thin dedicating time to a wide swath of random people, I invested in a small number of relationships that mattered to me. I surrounded myself with inspiration, encouragement, and support.

Third, I knew that in order to grow from this experience I needed a creative outlet or way to better connect with myself. I started a journal and began to practice things like gratitude and mindfulness. I also wrote myself the love letter you read in the **Accepting** section. I felt more in tune with my feelings than ever before.

As more time passed, the guys that I had been casually seeing slowly stopped texting. At first, the silence was deafening; I would reach for my phone just to see a blank screen with no notifications. But over time I grew to appreciate having more stillness in my life. I started creating new routines like stretching before bed or relaxing at night with a cup of herbal tea. I started cooking at home more often and saving money for my financial goals. (For once I actually *had* financial goals.) I also started working out and taking better care of my body. Instead of overexerting myself to the point of exhaustion, I got comfortable with the idea of missing a night out so that I could recharge.

It all boiled down to boundaries. I needed to set clear and conscious boundaries to reinstate a sense of safety, security, and self-trust. I needed to learn how to take care of myself again.

In the months after my detox was officially over, I felt my entire presence shift. I was more confident and open. I was lively and self-assured. I was more comfortable in my own skin than I had ever been before. I felt magnetizing to others. I attracted love—not just for the first time ever, but twice! I learned that I could let down my walls and allow others to truly know me—to cut through the noise of validation.

After taking a long, hard look at my life, I realized something quite profound: I was the common denominator in all of my experiences. If I really wanted to change, I had to be the one to actively choose to break the cycle. Awakening to this power inside, I finally started to see the distractions in my life for what they really were: Unnecessary noise standing in the way of my happiness. Filtering the diversions out for the first time allowed me to begin the process of re-discovering my true self buried under all the external validation upon which I had built my life. I certainly wasn't able to do that with a social calendar that offered something different every night of the week.

It can be really scary to think about stripping down to the essentials of your existence. We become attached to the way things are. Soon enough, letting go starts to feel impossible because we don't know what life is like on the other side of Change. You've picked up this book because you want to find your way. Don't be afraid to say no to someone else so you can say yes to yourself. Yes, you may miss out on some fun experiences. Yes, you may get bored. Yes, your fake friends might think you're lame. Yes, you'll be trading comfort for uncertainty. But you'll also start living a life that's authentic and actually means something to you. When we let go of our need for surface-level validation we make space for the deep fulfillment of vulnerability. Truth is, there's nothing more gratifying or real.

THE NEED TO BE NAKED

Love crept in and knocked on the door. And I finally answered.

I'll never forget the softness of our skin gently grazing, the sweet sweat of anticipation conjured in dewy palms. We stopped in front of an ornate church on a quiet side street in Midtown East as he mustered up the courage to speak his truth. "There's something I need to tell you, Chris," he said, eyes pointed down at the sidewalk.

He was facing me now and our four hands became two. He leaned in close, our noses just barely touching, before shifting over to my ear to whisper, "I love you" the way a pillowcase whispers its secrets to the night. He pulled his head back slowly and smiled softly as he continued revealing his feelings. "I've been in love with you since the day I met you. I know it hasn't been that long, but I just know. There's no denying it." My eyes filled with happiness as I leapt into his arms for a long embrace, then a prolonged, passionate kiss. It was Labor Day. The warmth of summer was slipping away and another warmth was taking its place in my heart.

Two weeks later it was my time to confess. After driving me home from an evening spent meeting his friends, we parked in an empty spot across from my apartment building in the Financial District. Daylight was fading and dusk was approaching. I shifted my body toward him as he sat in the driver's seat. The words ran out of my mouth, eager to be heard.

"I'm finally ready to tell you," I said, working up the courage to speak. "I undeniably, unequivocally, uncontrollably love you. I feel it in my core every time I look into your eyes, think of you, or say your name out loud." It was the first time I told a man I loved him.

I still had my seatbelt on, but I'd become unbuckled, open in a way I'd never been before, vulnerable for the very first time. He grabbed my hand and squeezed it as he leaned in to kiss me.

We walked arm-in-arm down to the water and reflected on the whirlwind of the previous few weeks where the seeds of love blossomed unexpectedly into something sacred, something pure. Time seemed to slow down and speed up all at once that night. Our love had been painted on my heart forever. The sweet serenity of reciprocity overtook me, basking me in a glow I'd never felt before. I was raw and revealed. I was stripped and sanctified. I was naked with all of my clothes on.

FOR THE FIRST TIME

Being seen for the first time is a watershed moment. When you allow yourself to be truly and deeply understood and known for who you really are, your hard drive writes over the painful memories in your mind and replaces them with moments of joy, vulnerability, and love. You finally see that you are capable of complete connection with another person. The worries of yore wither away. A mask tumbles to the ground after a dark and disillusioning masquerade. You decide to defy your shame stories, your samskaras, and your scripts. You are healed.

At least that's what happened to me. Hearing and speaking those three little words marked a momentous occasion for me because it proved beyond a shadow of a doubt that I was cherished, respected, and appreciated. Life suddenly didn't have to be defined by death or divorce or disorder. A flood washed it all away, leaving me cleansed. In its wake, I discovered lush kisses, endless laughs, and a lucky brand of love that was entirely mine and uniquely ours.

There are few things more satisfying and delightful than reciprocated vulnerability and affection. But that doesn't mean it's easy. This level of openness feels extremely risky because you are exposing parts of yourself that you've fought to keep hidden from plain view. You are defying the voice of fear and resistance inside that says you'll get hurt. You're jumping without a parachute.

But with high risk comes high reward. We cannot be fully seen by another unless we allow them to become fully aware of the shadows in our heart. This awareness is a beacon of light that dissipates the dark clouds within. A correction occurs when two souls recognize each other for the first time. This is what it means to truly love.

When I went through my detox, I made it my mission to eliminate shallow substitutes for connection in favor of real, soul-affirming love. I actively chose to let go of people, places, and things that were vapid, draining, and surface-level—that I felt took more than they gave back. Like clearing out the junk food and replacing it with fruits and veggies, I reinvested in what I knew would nourish me and help me grow. I reaped what I sowed.

> A correction occurs when two souls recognize each other for the first time. This is what it means to truly love.

I solidified my relationship with myself by standing up for and actively putting effort into what I knew was good for me. This is how I rebuilt the foundation of my life—my inner center of gravity. Spend some time reflecting on those areas of your life where you could use some pruning. Get it out on paper by jotting down all of the changes you've thought about making. Chances are, you likely know what you need to do. You may just need to get clear, organized, and prepared to dive in. The anticipation of these choices tends to be more difficult than the actual result of the choices themselves. Grant yourself the permission to choose. Try a little bit of change at a time so you can test and learn.

When it came time to turn outward and construct a house on top of my own foundation, I knew that I'd need the right crew by my side to create something sturdy, stable, and long lasting. I wanted people who knew all my flaws and loved me anyway. I craved connections that were just as devoted to me as I was to them. This was the beginning of my Circle of Trust.

THE CIRCLE OF TRUST

I'll always have a special place in my heart for Nashville, Tennessee.

"You should seriously come to Nashville with me next weekend to celebrate my 30th birthday!" My friend, Sarah Anne—also known as SAS—and I were on our second bottle of wine at a rooftop bar in Tribeca overlooking the Hudson River. The summer breeze was warm and, at this point, so was our rosé.

"Are you sure?" I asked, not wanting to overstep. "I've always wanted to go to Nashville and have never been." I was struggling to contain my excitement as I took another sip. I was newly unemployed and thrilled by the prospect of taking advantage of all the time off I had on my hands.

"Duh. My parents will love you!" SAS said, her excitement beginning to match mine. With the clink of our glasses, we solidified the trip—and our love for one another too.

A week and a half later, I was the first to arrive in Nashville. Sarah Anne's mom, Susan, welcomed me into their home with open arms and helped me get settled.

The next few days were replete with all sorts of adventures, each epic in their own right. There were several backyard barbecues. There was a rainbow bouncy house, complete with a slide and an inflatable pool. There was an epic sing-along to 90s music until 2 a.m. There were walkabouts and movies, thunderstorms and naps. There were several late nights spent talking with Sarah Anne about our goals and hopes and dreams. When I needed it most, I was reminded that being surrounded by people with whom you can be your authentic self is the best feeling in the world.

Nashville was one of the most transformational trips of my adult life. During that time of uncertainty and unemployment, I realized that I had a choice: I could feed into the self-doubt and the fear of trying to figure out my next step, or I could surrender to what's possible and become more myself in the process. Nashville was the first time in a long time that I chose the latter. That choice caused a shift in energy within me. I no longer cared what people thought about me or wanted me to do; I chose to embrace the freedom of just being unapologetically me. The conversations I had were deeper and more meaningful. People were more welcoming and open because *I* was more welcoming and open. The energy I put out into the humid Nashville summer air was being mirrored back at me—smiles, sweat, and all. And it was all a result of choosing to accept that invitation from Sarah Anne.

But the truth is, up until about a year before the trip to Nashville, SAS and I had never hung out one-on-one. The first time we did was a picture-perfect Sunday in May. Sarah Anne had just broken up with her boyfriend of several years, whom she was living with at the time. And she was looking for any excuse she could find to get out of the apartment. So I gave her one.

"Let's meet at the Starbucks on the corner of Broad and Beaver in an hour," I said.

Sarah Anne sat down at the table with her iced coffee and we instantly connected. We were both opening up to the possibility of one another.

"What's your next step?" I asked, trying to gauge where she was at emotionally.

"Well, first I need to find a new place to live. And then I think I need a dance party," she said with a sarcastic giggle. Even in the midst of one of the most difficult challenges she'd ever faced, Sarah Anne's spirit shined brighter than ever. At that point, we'd known each other for over four years and this was the first conversation of consequence we'd ever had.

"Name the place and I'm there," I said, hoping some music and quality time would help us become closer friends. "Honestly, there's nothing a little Mariah dance moment can't fix." We both laughed and nodded in agreement.

After a couple of hours of caffeine and conversation, I opened up to her: "I'm so glad we finally got to hang just the two of us. I'd really like to do it again soon." She agreed emphatically and we both left to head home, not knowing that there were bigger plans in store for us.

In the months leading up to the invitation to Nashville, Sarah Anne and I ran into each other at a mutual friend's birthday gathering in Brooklyn—and finally got our dance party.

"We must make plans and hang out soon," I said to her, repeating the same words she'd heard me utter more than a handful of times over the years. But this time I chose to follow through. I started texting Sarah Anne more often to see when she was available to meet up. Before I knew it, we were hanging out multiple times a month. I was choosing to spend my time with her—and she was choosing to reciprocate as well. All it took was a breakup, a birthday, and a bold leap of faith for us both, and a new best friendship was born. My Circle of Trust was irreversibly altered.

YOUR BOARD OF DIRECTORS

From a very young age, my dad instilled in me the importance of associating with people like SAS. "The people you surround yourself with have a huge impact on you, Son," he told me. "Choose your friends wisely."

Motivational speaker Jim Rohn advocated for a strong support system as well, stating that we're the average of the five people we spend the most time with. If that's true, then I'm more vulnerable because of Sarah Anne. I'm goofier because of Haley. I'm more free spirited because of Josh. I'm wittier because of Hunter. And I'm more appreciative because of Courtney. My choice to devote more time and energy to each of them was an investment in myself because they helped me step more fully into who I am.

Over the years, my friends have helped me feel seen, heard, and understood. They've encouraged me to pursue my dreams and reach my full potential. They've laughed, cried, and yelled with me. They've reminded me time and time again of what makes me special and what I have to offer the world. We've lifted each other up after rough breakups and unexpected deaths and countless obstacles. We've traveled the world together. We've shared our deepest secrets with each other. We're there for one another when we need it most. That kind of acceptance and emotional security is rare and special, and should be cherished. The truth about life is that it's difficult and lonely to get by on your own. With the right friends by your side, you don't have to. That starts with the people you choose to allow in your Circle of Trust.

Think about it: *Mean Girls* has the Plastics. *Queer Eye* has the Fab Five. Jesus has his 12 disciples. Come through, *Sisterhood of the Traveling Pants*. Everywhere you turn, the concept of a core group of friends is front and center. And it should come as no surprise: Friendship is one of the most important and enjoyable parts of life.

Your network helps you realize your net worth. All friendships are literal investments of your time and energy, and should help you to grow and become a better version of yourself than you could be on your own. Our friends complement us and help to shore us up in areas where we may lack strength. But if one friend shifts to become a source of deprivation instead of inspiration, it may be time to reconsider your investment and re-shuffle accordingly. Your Circle of Trust cannot be compromised. You may also be the source of deprivation for others, in which case they may reconsider their investment in you as well. It's always a two-way street.

Harmony is key. You need a mix of breadth and depth in your friend group. You need to give and receive aid from those friends. You need to be consistent and reliable in showing up for them and supporting them. And they need to do the same for you.

I like to think of my friends as the Board of Directors for my life. There are only a select number of spots available. In order to be given a spot on the Board, you have to demonstrate that you're dependable, honest, and loyal. Each person tapped to sit on the Board brings something different to the table—a unique blend of perspectives and a balanced set of qualities that help push me to be the best version of myself I can be. There are also occasional evaluations of the Board to ensure I have the right people in my corner and that my investments are sound.

Every friendship fulfills you in some way, but that fulfillment may not last forever. Your priorities can and will shift over time and cause you to not be on the same path as others anymore—and that's okay. I've let go of my fair share of friendships over the years. Some just faded away naturally because of physical distance. Others fell to the wayside because we grew apart. Still others ended because I realized we were no longer on the same path or headed in the same direction in life, and I made the choice to actively reallocate my energy elsewhere.

One of the healthiest things you can do in life is realize when something no longer serves the light in you. Give yourself permission to distance yourself from anything and anyone that no longer aligns with the best parts of who you are. I once heard that the Universe places people in your life for a reason, a season, or a lifetime. Learn to differentiate between the three and honor the presence of the people who join your journey, regardless of how short or long they may stay. People will come and go throughout your life. It's your job to focus on the people who continue to support and uplift you as you grow. As you strive to become a better version of yourself, your Circle of Trust will naturally evolve. These folks will walk the path of highest good right alongside you. Make sure you choose worthy travel companions.

Sarah Anne's presence in my life is a perfect example of the evolution of my Circle of Trust—of the evaluation of my Board of Directors. As the President of my life, I promoted her to the Board because she encouraged me to be genuinely myself and was sincere and active in supporting my happiness.

> One of the healthiest things you can do in life is realize when something no longer serves the light in you.

CHOOSING

Life is ultimately about the choices you make. I chose to meet Sarah Anne at that Starbucks. I chose to express to her that I wanted to be closer. I chose to reach out more. I chose to spend more time with her. I chose to go to Nashville.

And I'm choosing to tell you about all of it now so you can get brutally honest with yourself about your friend group. Start by making a list of all the people you consider to be your close friends. Reflect on how you keep in contact with them. Think about how often you see them in person. Also make a list of all the people around whom you feel that you can truly be yourself. How often do you see those people? Are there any discrepancies between your inner circle and the folks who bring out your authentic self? Take note of any opportunities to go deeper with either close friends or folks you'd like to be closer with. Also take note of friendships that might be stale, stagnant, or slipping away. How can you turn those particular friendships around? Write about the opportunities available for you to go deeper in developing your own personal Circle of Trust and Board of Directors. Keep in mind this Circle of Trust checklist as you write.

I will choose people for my Circle of Trust who:

- Lift me up and make me feel like I can be 100% me.
- Are open, honest, and communicative.
- Enjoy nights out just as much as nights in.
- Call me out on my B.S. but don't make me feel bad about it.

- Remind me that everything is going to be okay because they'll be there.
- Apologize when they're wrong and forgive me when I'm wrong, too.

I will choose to let go of those people in my life who:
- Are flakey, unreliable, and untrustworthy.
- Are incapable of maintaining my trust.
- Don't own up to their mistakes.
- Aren't able to follow through.
- Drag me down and only focus on the negative.
- Refuse to live with intention and purpose.
- Cause me more heartache than healing.

These two checklists can help you get clarity about where you stand with certain people in your life. If you find that more folks fall into the second list than the first, it may be time to revisit how you're allocating your time and energy.

A spot on your Board of Directors is a coveted role. This is rare earth we're talking about. It is earned through clear communication, consistent action, and unending support. When you're confident about who's in your corner, you know you can face any Change, overcome any obstacle, and triumph over any trauma. Find the courage within you to let go of connections that deprive you and choose ones that inspire you instead. It really does make all the difference.

FINALLY FREE

Choosing is a lighthouse of a different kind. It's not one you stumble upon by making it through perilous storms and rough seas; it's one you build to be the beacon in storms yet unseen.

Our choices reward us or cost us, help us evolve or devolve, push us forward or hold us back. When we choose to construct lighthouses, we aren't saying that we'll never encounter another tempest. We're declaring that we know there are tempests left untold and we'll be prepared when the rain and wind lash us with the familiar wetness of Change.

Purposefully, carefully, and righteously selecting what's in our best interests, aligned with our most noble values, and in tune with our path of highest good puts us back on the right track and brings us back home. This course correction is not accidental; it is intentional.

We make a lot of choices in life. If we slow down long enough to become aware of our actions, we can make decisions that are in line with our higher morals and motives. The more aware you are of the choices you make, the better those choices become. What's chosen peacefully in light won't drown you in the war of darkness. The two cannot coexist.

The two main choices we make pertain to our inner world and our outer orbit. We cultivate our inner world by challenging our automatic negative thoughts, rewriting our limiting beliefs, and clarifying our purpose. We shape our outer orbit by living in accordance with our inner world—picking friends, romantic partners, and vocations that support our virtues, values, and highest good.

Together, these choices stitch together a fabric of support that lifts us higher when we are low. This safety net pulls us back when we start to wander from our path—subvert, sabotage, or sacrifice ourselves with our choices. We are finally known and seen and understood. We are brought back home. We are free.

5
Embracing

HOW WILL YOU RESPOND?

A pack of stickers transformed my entire outlook on life.

While waiting in line to get into an event during Gay Pride in Washington, D.C., I met a woman covered in countless colorful stickers. After paying her a compliment, she removed one of the stickers from her face and placed it on mine. Then she offered me a pack of the same stickers she had delicately placed all over. Touched by her act of kindness, I enthusiastically accepted.

As we neared the front of the line and entered the venue, I grew increasingly uncertain of what to do with the stickers. But then my intuition whispered to me in a moment of clarity. *Offer a sticker to each person you see*, it implored. The simplicity and sincerity of this direction just felt *right*, so I decided to pass out stickers to anyone who was interested in one.

What happened next surprised me. I made my way around the room, approaching every single patron who was present. I kicked off each conversation with a "Happy Pride!" and tacked on a straightforward question at the end: "Would you like a flirty sticker to celebrate?" The responses I received moved me. Almost every single interaction was warm, friendly, and congenial. Many folks, after hearing that the stickers were free and there was absolutely no ulterior motive behind their distribution, requested multiple stickers or pulled aside other friends to be emblazoned with stickers of their own. When asked about my reasons for passing out the stickers, I explained how the kindness of a stranger inspired me to pass it on in the spirit of Pride. I also imparted that I felt it was important for us all to crush our comfort zones, break out of our bubbles, and cast aside our cliques in order to truly listen to one another and have meaningful conversations. "How are we supposed to change the world if we don't change how we show up in it?" I asked. "I'm just trying to spread a little love in the time I have left here on this planet," I said.

I met many magnificent souls that day. There was an older gentleman who showed up solo because he had no one with whom to celebrate Pride. He told me that the sticker made his loneliness subside for a second. I introduced him to another group I met earlier and he ended up making some friends. He gave me a kiss on the cheek as a show of thanks.

Later on in the evening, I happened upon a White House staffer. He graciously accepted a sticker and described his despair in dealing with the gay community in D.C. because of his affiliation with a certain political party and the particular President for whom he worked. I made space for his woes by listening carefully and intently, honoring the isolation and rejection he had experienced from members of his own community, whom he hoped would see him as more than his beliefs or his job. "Your demeanor and our conversation have given me hope for America," he said. We hugged as he left.

The stickers eventually ran out. But the lessons I learned that day are stickers of a different kind—momentous memories stuck to my soul as little reminders of what life is like when you live with an open heart. I was shown firsthand how kindness and empathy can disarm anyone and dislodge any hatred. I watched as people lit up with pure joy at the gift of a simple sticker. I learned that it's not about *what* you give; it's about *how* it's given. I finally understood the incontrovertible compassion that unlocks the human heart.

It's so easy to let life harden you—to shut down at the very moment life asks us to show up. Ask yourself: *When is the last time I didn't shy away from an opportunity life put in front of me?* We can choose not to close ourselves off or isolate ourselves. We can choose to pay attention to what's right in front of us. We can decide to open our cliques and our hearts ever so slightly for something new or someone different to enter.

The end of closing is the beginning of opening. The death of the ego becomes the rebirth of the soul. We unlock these levels inside us by choosing to push deeper within, holding a flashlight of inquisitive kindness up to our shadows. This exploration is an act of love. Instead of staying politely perched and shallowly surviving, we can be intimately involved and optimistically open. An activation of the heart occurs every time we allow ourselves to do this—to rediscover the well of love that lies underneath all of our attempts to preserve and protect ourselves. This realization jolts us alive.

Staying open to Change is what life is all about. When you live your life this way you will come to know this as the truth. Every time I stop trying to advance my agenda and pursue my own notion of how life should be, I'm able to show up for whomever and whatever most needs me at this moment. Even if it appears as a pack of radiant stickers and a room full of complete strangers.

These days, I look for these assignments and accept them as blessings in disguise. *What is life asking of me right now?* I inquire. *How can I show up more fully at this moment?* This is my new guidepost for a rich existence—a wealth beyond my own measure. I pay very close attention to what is being asked of me at any given moment and I ask more of my life, too. *How can I be of service? How can I give even more than I already am? How can I open my heart just a little wider?* I look for signs and listen for whispers in response to my inquiries. They don't always show up how I expect, but I accept them regardless because I've made it a priority to live life in this manner.

My heart is always fullest when it's wide open—when I relinquish my expectations and allow the Universe to use me as an instrument of love and a force of light. It's remarkable how transcendent an experience this is. The linchpin to a fulfilling, joyful life is simply having the courage to live it each and every second. All you have to do is have the nerve to heed this call. And to peel back the fear that surrounds your heart so it may answer. No matter *what* is being asked of you, it's *how* you show up that matters. The question is: How will you respond?

My heart is always fullest when it's wide open—when I relinquish my expectations and allow the Universe to use me as an instrument of love and a force of light.

DEFIANTLY OPEN

Our journey thus far has taken us where few have brazenly ventured before: Into the untouched wilderness within. We've explored what it looks like to resist—to step away from the path of light by subverting our spiritual journey and avoiding the fundamental experience of Change. We've traversed misty mires and stormy seas to reach a state of radical acceptance, coming to terms with the past that we felt broke us but in fact shaped us. We've examined our inner world and outer orbit to consciously choose the energy we allow into our lives. This has been an expedition of paring down, stripping back, and peeling away—of learning not to close our minds or hearts when things don't go according to our plan. But what should we do when Change shows up in another way, dressed in different robes, with the same flavor of fear? As a constant reminder of the flow and flux of the entire Universe, we should accept it at face value and befriend it. We should welcome Change wholeheartedly into our homes, our hearts, and our arms—embracing all the pain and struggle and plot twists. We are meant to remain defiantly open.

Keeping an open mind and an open heart is a choice we make consciously in order to learn from Change, to honor this fundamental law of life. But while Change may show up in myriad ways, we remain open as the result of seven sacred steps:

1. Realize everything is unfolding *for* you, not happening *to* you.
2. Never close your heart.

3. Honor your growth.

4. Heed the signs that you're where you need to be.

5. Know that the Universe's default is love.

6. Always act out of the power of your light.

7. Have faith that you'll be given equal or better.

These steps complete your journey back home. They will deliver you back to the path of highest good when you feel lost. Stop closing your heart and start opening it instead. Then recognize that you are a living, breathing, conscious being. Next, realize that you are not defined by the events that have occurred or will occur to you because you were, are, and will be the same essence of energy throughout those events. In embracing their death, you are accepting your life. After that, cultivate a belief that the Universe is a friendly place replete with love. Stand in the power of your light by refusing to react to the darkness in another. And always believe that you're being guided to something better.

This is how you come to terms with your past. This is how you surmount your pain in the present. This is how you embrace Change in the future. This is the final way to realize *it's good to see me again.*

UNFOLDING FOR YOU

I'm here to share an important reminder of your value in this world. As long as you remember this truth, you will have mastered what it means to truly live. This fundamental fact might confound you in its simplicity. Nevertheless, it is the key to all that life and Change have to offer. It is summed up in seven simple words: *Everything that happens is for your benefit.* All of the pain, all of the hurt, all of the heartbreak—it taught you something, it demonstrated that you can survive the darkness, it brought you back to the safe sands of home.

Every breath you take is a beloved reminder of the blessing of life that has been bestowed upon you and which comes to know itself through you. When I'm stressed out or anxious about what's going on around me, all I have to do is focus on the bountiful energy within me to remember that life is good because I am still here. It doesn't matter what a given day may throw at me; peace is only ever a breath away. When I let go of my need for life to be a certain way in order to be happy, I unlock the happiness that already exists within me. When I surrender my illusion of control, I am overcome with gratitude that God has given me another day. When I let go of my resistance and embrace reality as it is, magic manifests in my life. Everything I ask for is granted to me in equal or greater measure than I ever imagined it could be. It rarely shows up as I expected it would, but it eventually shows up regardless.

The following example is proof enough for me. A couple of years ago, I clarified my intention regarding my life's purpose. As I mentioned in the **Choosing** section, I realized that my gift lies in my ability to use words to impact others. I also knew my gift wasn't just limited to writing, either. Deep down, I wanted to become a motivational speaker as well—to use the power of words to touch an audience through verbal storytelling. While the steps to become a writer came easily to me, I was perplexed by how to break into the public speaking industry. But I believed in my intention and kept the faith. I felt in my core that I would be given the resources I needed to succeed so long as I remained committed to the vision and used my gifts as a means to help others. And then I was shown a sign. When a few close friends came to New York from Nashville for the week, they assembled a last-minute dinner party. There were a few new faces there. After getting to know one of the women a little better, I discovered that she worked for a firm that represented keynote speakers. *No way*, I thought. *The Universe is working its magic again!*

A few weeks later, when she came back to New York for work, she invited me to a small speaker symposium she organized on behalf of her company, and I cleared my schedule in order to attend. I watched in awe as two speakers presented their keynotes with eloquence, candor, and flair. Both of them were around my age, and I kept seeing similarities between their storytelling styles and mine. Their energy was infectious and only further reinforced my desire to get up in front of a large audience and bare my soul. I spoke to both of them after the event to tell them about my aspirations and was encouraged to stay the course and keep at it. I gushed to my new friend about how inspired I was to pursue public speaking and how I was so grateful that we met. We hugged and I headed home.

As I was walking to the elevator, I had an opportunity to talk with a couple of the booking agents who attended the symposium.

I told them about my journey with my blog, my progress in writing this book, and my desire to share my experiences as a means to help others heal. They were moved by my story and told me they wouldn't be surprised if they booked me one day, shaking my hand as we emptied out into a warm autumn evening.

I made my way up the street in the middle of rush hour, my gait a little slower and my smile a little wider than usual. The Universe showed me that you get what you have the clarity to ask for—that if you offer up a pure, loving intention and surrender the outcome, it will be granted to you in time. Faith isn't just born in grand moments where life seems to split at the seams; faith is also made resolute through the unwavering belief that, even in the most mundane of moments, life is unfolding for your benefit.

> When I let go of my need for life to be a certain way in order to be happy, I unlock the happiness that already exists within me.

Here's another example that life is happening for your ultimate benefit. Remember the story I shared about being let go from my job? Hearing that news was heartbreaking in every sense of the word. While I was able to dig deep and ask empowering questions, I also felt disillusioned. I questioned my worth. I wondered whether I'd find my footing again. I doubted my abilities. Even after many years of experience, I feared that my career had peaked when I was only 30 years old. Looking back with perspective several years later, I can truthfully say that being laid off is one of the best things to ever happen to me. I'm happier and more fulfilled now than I was then. I live a life that is aligned with my values and that allows me to be of service to others through the power of words and shared experiences. What I once perceived as a burden to bear eventually became one of the biggest blessings made manifest for my bright benefit.

No matter what, the Universal force of life will always try to course-correct back to the frequency of love—to the path of highest good. A lot of times, we misinterpret these course corrections because they don't align with our expectations. But they always show up and they are always for your ultimate benefaction.

Life doesn't happen *to* you. Life is the energetic force of consciousness that manifests *through* you. How, then, can it happen *to* you if it *is* you? It is impossible. You come to realize that life happens *for* you instead of *to* you when you remember that you and life are one in the same. If life is an ongoing conversation with Change, then you are the dialogue—the wondrous words that convey its meaning. You are the story and Life is the author. You have the free will to choose the *what*—the specific adventures that comprise the setting, the plot, and the characters. But the biggest adventure of all is *how* you're able to choose in the first place—the gift of awareness that was plucked from the Universal substrate and which powers your very existence. The fact that your story is still being written is testament to the fact that it matters—that it's unfolding for you. You've been granted a runway. It's up to you whether you spend your time taxiing or whether you take off. The only difference between the two is that the former thinks it's an engine and the latter knows it has wings.

As long as you're focused on growth, nothing can ever hold you back. The particular lessons themselves aren't as important as your willingness to learn them. When you live openly in this way, you become unshakably strong. Emotional earthquakes will eventually show up in one form or another. But they will always subside if you allow yourself to sit through them and appreciate the opportunity to learn from them—to sway with the motion of the ground until it shakes out new depths within you.

I don't know your life story. I'm not acutely aware of the trauma you've been through. But we've all experienced it. We've all felt burned by the flames of the past. We've all gone through our fair share of emotional earthquakes and spiritual reckonings. Here's what I can tell you beyond a shadow of a doubt: Everything you've ever endured was ultimately for your benefit. I believe you've been led to these words because you need to hear this reminder. Perhaps the way you've been approaching life is unhealthy, unconscious, and unsustainable. You're reading this book to find a way to somehow let go, move on, and start a new chapter. I know because I've lived it; I've been there. I was willing to do whatever it took, and I'm sure you are too. That's why I'm here to tell you to trust that there is a path for you, that you are being called back to it by being called through whatever circumstances you've had to surmount.

Everything in your life has led you to this point, to the rediscovery of the truth of who you are: A Universal incarnation that is inherently worthy because you exist. There isn't always a reason or a meaning behind the painful events in our lives. At least, it's rarely what we think it is. Honestly, it doesn't really matter. All that matters is that you're still taking another breath, learning another lesson. The rest is all just conjecture.

LET YOUR HEART BREAK

It was the wound I never intended to create.

While doing dishes early one summer Saturday, Change came knocking once again—this time in the form of a seemingly innocent pint glass. After washing the glass and placing it on the drying towel next to the sink, it became unstable and tipped over. Not wanting to break or damage any other dishes in the sink, I quickly reached my hand over to catch it. The force of my hand shattered the pint against the edge of the quartz counters, slicing my left ring finger open as a result.

I watched in disbelief as blood gushed from the gash in my finger. I immediately grabbed a bundle of paper towels and inspected the wound for any sign of glass. And then I did what any sensible thirty-something would do: I called my dad. Taking his advice, I walked to the nearest urgent care, hand held high to keep the blood from flowing to it.

An immediate wave of regret washed over me as I waited to see a doctor. *Why didn't I just let the glass break?* I thought. *If I hadn't tried to save it, I would've spared myself a ton of pain.* I spent a few minutes in this disempowering spiral until I heard my name called by an assistant and I snapped out of it. Four stitches and hundreds of dollars later, I returned home, shaken and startled but on the mend.

In life, glasses aren't the only things to shatter. Sometimes it takes the form of a broken bone during a soccer game. Other times it looks like friendships that drift apart or homes that become torn in two. Truth is there's a million ways the heart can break. But there's only one way it's made new again. And that's by *allowing* it to break in the first place. Whenever we try to protect ourselves from feeling pain—to prevent the hurt and heartbreak of Change from consuming us—we cause more suffering in the process because we're resisting the truth of reality. When we disavow reality in this way, we disavow our feelings, our assignments, and ourselves. Please hear me clearly when I say this: Your heart will shatter regardless of whether or not you try to salvage it. It's just a matter of whether you'll allow it to shatter everything else in the process.

There is another approach. You can quit walking through life with a hidden layer of bubble wrap. You can take off the armor. You can actually let your heart break. Over the years, I tried every way imaginable to stop my heart from falling apart. I ran away from anything that made me uncomfortable. I avoided the truth. I buried my feelings as far down as they'd go. I numbed myself. But not only did none of it work, it only exacerbated the pain in the process.

I didn't realize it at the time, but I wasn't breaking down; I was breaking open. I wasn't falling apart; I was falling together. Contrary to what you may believe, your heart never breaks and dies; your heart breaks and is reborn. Like a phoenix triumphantly rising from the ashes, your heart is renewed through breaking, shattering, and crumbling. This is how we open ourselves back up to the world, to our feelings, to the full spectrum of possibility.

Heartbreak, then, is a cathartic experience. It knocks down the walls that lock away our love. It disintegrates the chains that bind us. It casts out the shadows as we are carefully put back together in light. Heartbreak should really be called *heartbirth*. Another chapter starts, another page is turned, another era begins. If **Resisting** manifests as heartbreak, then **Embracing** manifests as heartbirth. While the former is damaging and destructive, the latter is restorative and replenishing. Embracing your heartbreaks as heartbirths will completely change your outlook, your perspective, and your life. It'll open you up to miracles and welcome all that's meant for you.

A closed heart is a black hole. It will consume your entire life. This feels like a prison to a spirit that's boundless. It simply can't escape the gravitational pull. But an open heart is a beaming star. It illuminates everything it touches with light. It creates order out of chaos. It pulls planets and moons into orbit and gives them a home. It is the definition of heaven within.

Living with a wide-open heart is my new life creed. Even if it feels like it's been broken in the process, I know it'll mend again. Because it can never really break, it can only be born. And the love it contains and the wisdom I've gained can never be destroyed, no matter how many times it shatters. My only goal now is to let it.

THE SECOND TIME AROUND

In my Philosophy 101 class in college, I wrote a paper on the logical plausibility of time travel. In that paper, I tackled the Second Time Around Fallacy, which states that there can be no set of circumstances in which a series of events unfold in one way the first time around and then in another way the second time around. Basically, if it happened one way in the past, it has always and will always happen that way. In the context of time travel, the person traveling back would've already been present the first time around, therefore negating any possibility of there being a Second Time Around.

I think the same is true of our emotional or spiritual lives. We can mentally recount and revisit what has happened to us—we can travel back in time, so to spreak—but we cannot change what actually happened.

In that sense, I've traveled back in time on more occasions than I care to admit. I've replayed every interaction with my mom to think of how I could've saved her. I've second-guessed every moment with Michele, wondering what I would've done differently if I'd just believed I could've. I've recapped every failed relationship in my head to see where it could have possibly gone wrong. Yet the past still remains the same. But I do not. I've progressed to a state of higher awareness, to a level from which I can see more clearly. This perspective is further removed, more objective, and easier from which to evaluate. We are not fixed points on a line. The experiences of our lives have the power to propel us further along, higher up, and more deeply inside than we ever imagined we'd venture.

Once you've been spiritually awakened—that is to say consciously aware and propelled to this level—you'll never look at anything the same way again. Suddenly, the world is a place full of possibility, vibrancy, and love. People and places that bothered you no longer hold any weight over you. The ego-driven drama and pettiness of your former life become meaningless. The world hasn't changed, but your existence within it certainly has. You're no longer a bystander in the beautiful story that is your life. You are present and seeing things with a new vision. Your life becomes split into before and after finding this new footing.

A spiritual awakening is like a cleansing rain. It is a baptism in its own right—a moment of pure but ephemeral self-actualization. These moments of distillation add up over time until our resistance is washed away and we see things with a renewed sense of clarity. The darkness of the unconscious mind tries to trap us again and again. The decision to remain rooted in the light of our awareness is how we cleanse these dark thoughts and finally see again.

The Second Time Around is a journey of gaining this perspective—of purifying our perceptions of the past. We start to see the same old events of our lives in a different way and in a new light. The circumstances remain the same, but your position relative to them changes. You're no longer concerned with trying to alter the event or make it anything other than what it was. You're not triggered and outraged by the casual observation of the occurrence itself. You are graciously perched above the perilous storms that once waged, looking down on them from a place of higher consciousness. This space is sacred. As we learned in the **Accepting** section, recognizing that we must accept what can't be changed gives us the foundation to step into this higher ground—to a place of peace that's granted to us by the serenity to radically accept what we can't control. The Second Time Around is a way to radically accept what you can't change in your life. When something comes up that brings you back to a traumatic moment in time, you are no longer burned by or enslaved to it. You are quiet and calm, reverent for what it taught you, and gracious for the growth you've achieved. This is a tremendous accomplishment. Healing is messy work. You don't turn inward without getting your hands dirty in the muck. But this is how we decontaminate our minds.

I might not be done traveling back in time. You might not be either. One thing I am through with is trying to do anything about it. I no longer have any interest in resisting the laws of nature that cannot be broken. These days, when I look back, it's always with gratitude, compassion, and thankfulness. After all, the pain of the past didn't erode me—it built me into the man I am today. And that ain't no crying shame.

THE POWER OF LOVE

Life is never silent. It is anything but. Its sole mission is to make you more aware—to help you connect to the precious and indestructible force within you that powers all living things. It does this in many ways, but one of the most profound and often overlooked is through signs. Remember, life is a conversation with Change. When the status quo or energy of a situation shifts, it is telling you to follow—to become aware of Change and act from the seat of this awareness.

We've talked a lot about how life speaks to you, but it also works the other way around. Since you and life are one in the same, you can easily converse with this force of Universal presence. I do it all the time through prayer, meditation, visualization, and other techniques. The same energy that powers the heavens flows through you as well. Thus, the Universe is always open to co-creating with you if you so choose. This intimate connection to spirit is unlimited and available to everyone. I constantly co-create with the Universe. First, I think of an intention. *What do I intend to do here?* I ask. Sometimes, this is fast and fleeting—a passing thought in a flowing stream of consciousness. Other times, this process is slow and willful, and full of deliberate direction. No matter which form it takes, I proceed to the next step, where I make a request based on my intention. The key here is to remember that no request is too small if your intentions are pure. Next, I surrender the outcome and believe wholeheartedly that it will show up for me eventually. Again, sometimes I don't even realize I'm doing this and other times it is preconceived and purposeful. I concentrate on accepting my own worthiness and fulfillment, and I allow that to envelop me. This unwavering faith allows me to release my expectation while assuming the energetic feeling of already possessing what I intend to manifest. Finally, I stay vigilant for signals from the Universe that I'm on the right path—that I'm right where I need to be. I pay attention to what, when, and how things manifest in my life and I heed the signs I'm being guided by a higher force. This process works wonders, so let me spell it out clearly for you:

- Get clear about your intention.
- Make a request based on that intention.
- Surrender the outcome.
- Channel the feeling of already having what you desire.
- Look for signs.

Here's one example where the process worked for me. I once went on a trip to Miami to celebrate my birthday with my friend Sarah Anne. A few weeks prior to the trip, a friend of a friend I met on a previous trip to Miami popped into my mind. I always have the intention of connecting with kindhearted and good-natured people, and this person was no exception. *I wonder what he's up to these days*? I pondered. I casually thought about reaching out to him via social media but never got around to it. Once the inclination to reach out had passed, I unconsciously and unintentionally surrendered the outcome to the Universe.

After dinner on our second night in Miami, Sarah Anne and I made our way to one of our favorite bars. As soon as we walked in the door, I came face to face with the same friend that had popped into my mind weeks earlier. Come to find out, he had moved away from Miami and was back visiting with his boyfriend, who had never been to Miami before. I mentioned to him that I had recently thought of him, and it turned out that he had thought of me, too. We snapped a photo and sent it to the mutual friend who introduced us years ago as we reminisced on old times and exchanged stories on how our lives had unfolded since we'd last seen each other. Since the trip, we've kept in closer contact. I'm not certain there was any deeper meaning to the encounter. I don't know what the chances are of us running into one another in a city in which neither of us lives. All I know is that I made a request of the Universe and it was clearly answered—that I was shown I was right where I needed to be. It's signs like this that humble me and show me beyond a shadow of a doubt that the Universe is listening. Even when I'm not speaking all that loudly.

On that same trip to Miami, yet another sign showed up for me. This time was a little different, because my request was specific, and there was no mistaking its appearance as a guidepost from God. The morning after running into my friend, a thought popped into my head. I rolled over in my bed and shared the thought as a good morning greeting to Sarah Anne: "This is so incredibly random, but I really want to hear *The Power of Love* by Celine Dion right now." We both laughed. My request was offered up and surrendered to the powers that be.

Later on that afternoon, while passing a clothing boutique a block away from our hotel, I noticed a familiar song playing on the speakers. It was *The Power of Love* by Celine Dion. I stood in the middle of the sidewalk and turned to Sarah Anne, both of us speechless and in disbelief. The second we walked away, the song changed mid-chorus. We caught it just in time as we were walking by, the odds of the encounter not lost on either of us. We were both blown away by the guidance available to us. I smiled from ear to ear at the direct reassurance I received from the Universe in that moment.

Whether it's a chance encounter with a friend who crossed your mind, a favorite song that plays for a fleeting moment as you walk by a boutique, or something else entirely, this is meant to show you that a higher power is always listening to you. Maybe you believe in God. Maybe you call it by another name like the Universe. Maybe you simply know it as a force with no name at all. Regardless of labels, energy of the highest order is always at your disposal. It's just a matter of whether you ask it to show you that it's there. For me, these moments of synchronicity are reminders of the love and guidance available to me at all times. I take them seriously and make a point of noticing when they show up. And I follow them. I know in my soul that they're a form of encouragement that I'm right where I need to be—and that I'm living my life with an open heart. All I have to do is just ask. The Universe will do the rest. That's the real *Power of Love*.

FRIENDLY OR HOSTILE?

There's a quote that inspires my way of looking at the world, my feelings toward humanity, and my relationship with life itself. Often attributed to famed physicist Albert Einstein, this quote powers the nature of my existence and my relation to Universal Consciousness. "The most important decision we make is whether we believe we live in a friendly or hostile universe."

These words transformed my life in two triumphant ways. First, they helped me clarify how I observe the events I experience. In the past, when I perceived Change as unpleasant, it would put me into a tailspin and cause me to resist, complain, and go into fight-or-flight mode. Now, I do my best not to rush to judgment or jump to conclusions because I recognize that the Universe is friendly, and thus all situations—painful or not—have valuable information that I can use to make decisions that are more conscious and purposeful, and in harmony with my values. In short, I recognize that I can't control *what* unfolds in my life, but I always have the power to consciously choose *how* I respond. Regardless of what happens I will always retain that power. Instead of believing that life is acting against me or for my detriment, sweeping me up in its grasp and refusing to let me go, I can choose to interpret what I deem to be unfavorable events as guideposts toward a friendlier, more loving place—often to my chagrin but always for my ultimate benefit.

This is about the purpose or role something plays in the bigger picture of our lives. As cognitive beings, it's only natural that we desire to know what something means, though we're often shortsighted and myopic in our interpretation of the circumstances since we're approaching any given situation with a clear set of expectations, a deeply-nuanced bank of experiences and memories, and a sensitive storage unit of scripts and samskaras that we've been conditioned to believe will play out in a preconceived and predictable manner. We are beings of Change and are defined by our relationship with it. The Friendly Universe perspective helps characterize and contextualize both the changes we witness and the emotional pain we endure as a result of those changes. Despite how painful a situation might feel at the time, seeing life as a force of creation instead of destruction and an energy of humility instead of hostility helps us rise out of the moment to understand the events of our lives with the perspective of a Higher Order. Ultimately, I see everything that happens as a signal to fear less and love more. Knowing that I exist within the context of a friendly and loving Universe helps me do just that.

The other way the discovery of this quote helped me live a better life is that it reinstated a sense of safety within me. Knowing deep down that we live in a friendly Universe helped me give up resisting and practice acceptance instead. For a long time, I thought the Universe was torturing me—that I was being subjected to pain and suffering that no one else had to deal with. But this quote helped me to challenge and ultimately change that perspective, guiding me to see another possibility: Perhaps the only hostility that was present was the way I was looking at the Universe, and not the way the Universe was treating me after all. Looking at reality as a realm of potential instead of pandemonium, I can see beyond what's happening on a day-to-day basis and raise myself up out of the shadows with the understanding that it doesn't matter *what* happens, if *how* I see it is through the lens of love, kindness, and compassion. Because I know these are the organizing principles of the entire Universe.

I sense that the Universe and everything within it default to that same principle of possibility, of which love is the purest and most noble expression. Our Universe is full of miracles, replete with blessings, and ripe with the expansiveness of love. Look no further than a nebula of cradled stars or a stellar supernova to see heavenly proof of this sweeping growth. Even when it's disguised as destruction, it is still a form of creation. These are naturally-occurring phenomena, part of the cycle of life and the way things are. It's when we interfere with small-minded thinking and closed-hearted conditioning that we turn the Universe on its head. Underneath what we perceive to be chaos and calamity, there is a beautiful order that permeates all things. It's a layer of benevolence that exists beyond the boundaries of our limited senses, selfish tendencies, and insular interests. You reach this point of understanding when you give up thinking that the Universe is nefarious and learn to see it as good-natured instead.

> I see everything that happens as a signal to fear less and love more.

The truth is that the Universe, like all entities and energies, doesn't operate by our limited standards of duality—of hostility or friendliness. It is probably both and neither at the same time, depending on how you look at it. But if I'm going to invest in a belief system, I'd rather it be permeated by optimism, openness, and potential rather than riddled with pessimism, futility, and limitations.

Wouldn't you?

THE NEW GOLDEN RULE

Early on in life, my dad reinforced the necessity of The Golden Rule. "Do unto others as you would have them do unto you," he said when I was faced with a physical confrontation or emotional dilemma. After hearing it enough times, it became ingrained in my mind—a key component of my value structure that informed how I behaved and how I interpreted the behavior of others.

The Golden Rule is just that: A universally accepted standard that shows us how to remain golden in all our interactions. This standard practice is meant to help you empathize with another's position. When I think about whether or not I'd want someone else to treat me in the same manner I'm treating them, it helps me gain perspective and return to a state of compassion if I've fallen out of alignment with what is of the highest good. But, while fundamental and universal, there's one aspect that's not predicted by The Golden Rule: What should you do if the other person doesn't treat you how they'd like to be treated?

The Golden Rule is predicated on the ability of both parties to treat the other with veneration and careful consideration. When this unspoken agreement is violated by one person in the situation, the moral agreement breaks down, causing a gap to appear. Thus, we tend to treat others how we *feel* we've been treated, not how we'd actually *like* to be treated. Retaliation and reaction are the real impulses that drive our behavior, not the ideals of The Golden Rule.

Here's an example from my life. On New Year's Eve a few years ago, I got into a disagreement while messaging with one of my best friends. One thing led to another and before I knew it the argument escalated and the conversation broke down. I was still feeling hurt a few days later when he reached out to make amends. I didn't feel that the moral gap had been adequately bridged and I failed to communicate that feeling, which led to a falling out that left us contactless for nearly a year. Silence and time filled the physical gap that formed in place of the perceived moral one.

In the months that followed, I thought a lot about the situation and how I could've handled it better—how I would've shown up in a more mature and loving way had I slowed down long enough to be intentional in my actions. Because of the experience, I devised what I dubbed **The New Golden Rule**: Always act out of the power of your light instead of allowing others to trigger your darkness.

The key is to always meet the darkness with light instead of more darkness, ego, and fear. Do not let others lead you astray and trap you in a situation that does not reflect your core values. This will help to ensure that you don't just react to what happens to you. No matter what comes your way, you will meet each situation with precisely the same approach and energy. Your character and integrity will be intact despite how much your own darkness and ego—and the darkness and ego of others—may try to distract you. You will be fiercely spiritually sound.

The New Golden Rule is a reflection of what we know to be true and right and paramount. Just because someone treats you in an undesirable way does not mean you should fall into the perceived moral gap that emerges in your mind. This updated paradigm reasserts your ability to consciously choose as opposed to being unconsciously triggered. The key here is to learn to cast the light of your awareness on the energy that arises within you. Be curious. Train yourself to pause for a period of nonjudgmental evaluation. During this brief but pivotal pause, you can choose whether you will keep an open heart and allow the energy to pass through, or whether you will resist the energy, close your heart, and interrupt the natural flow of things.

Bottom line: When you become aware enough to notice your energy shift because of a perceived moral gap, you can pause to reflect before you respond. You reclaim your power to choose when you stay firmly rooted in this acute state of awareness. There's no greater mastery of self than being aware of your triggers and taking back your control. That's the essence of **The New Golden Rule**.

In the end, the way we treat another person is just a reflection of how we feel about ourselves. This is why the light of awareness is so important. Instead of reacting from a place of fear or insecurity, you can preemptively reach out a helping hand and say, "Are you okay? You're not acting like yourself right now." Rather than allowing one domino to make all of the others fall, you can stand firm in your awareness and not be tipped over into the darkness that's been thrust upon you.

These days, when I see someone who's angry or acting out, I don't see the presence of darkness; I see the absence of light. This reminds me of the concept of Namaste, which is commonly interpreted as "the light in me sees the light in you." When perceived moral gaps arise, we can make the conscious choice to look for the light in another. And look past the rest.

Nearly a year after our falling out, I sent a Christmas card to my best friend. "One of the things that always brought us closer was our fair share of traumatic experiences from the past," I wrote before confessing and apologizing. "I fear that the way things went down between us triggered us both—and perhaps echoed some of those painful memories. For that and so much more, I am sincerely sorry. I needed a lot of time and space to myself this past year to heal on my own. I hope that at some point, you and I may heal our friendship as well." An olive branch of light was extended. There were no longer any gaps—perceived or not. There were just two people who loved each other and wanted to make amends. We were on our way to being golden again.

THE EQUAL OR BETTER PRINCIPLE

A friend of mine once told me that when you converse with the Universe it only has three potential answers: *Yes, not yet,* or *something better is on its way.*

When I heard this, I was taken aback. *The Universe doesn't say no?* I wondered in my mind, thinking over all the times I believed my prayers had gone unanswered when in reality there were bigger plans in store for me.

This initially shocked me. But then I had an epiphany: The Universe doesn't have to say no. When one branch of possibility gets cut off, several more sprout in new directions to replace it. The Universe wants to see me thrive and be at peace in this form. And it will do everything in its almighty power to make that my reality as long as I have faith that it is working on my behalf—as long as I have the clarity to see those other branches appear, and believe that they will get me where I'm meant to go.

This is the essence of what I like to call the **Equal or Better Principle**: Even if it's hard as hell, even if it looks nothing like you imagined it would, even if it takes longer than you expect, you are always guided to something better because you are granted the opportunity to learn, to grow, and to heal. The important thing to accept about Change is that it often takes you by surprise, but it also whisks you away to destinations that you wouldn't have arrived at on your own. This is the Universe's way of shielding you from what's not meant for you. Thus, redirection is a form of protection—a way to gently maneuver you to other opportunities that will be more fruitful for your growth.

The Equal or Better Principle has three main components: Awareness, trust, and growth. The first component of the Equal or Better Principle is awareness. Awareness comes first because it is how you can recognize that this principle has already played an active role in your life. You survived things you never thought you would. Each earth-shattering moment and every heartbirthing experience eventually subsided to give way to brighter days. All along you were led to better. You traversed trauma and bounced back stronger and wiser. You always outlasted.

Trust is the second component of the Equal or Better Principle. In order for this principle to really work for you, you need to believe that, just like before, you will be transported to bigger, brighter, and better experiences. Despite the way things might look during difficult times, try not to succumb to the voice of fear inside that tells you that it will last forever. You know that it won't because you've been shown that it won't many times before. Have faith that this time will be no different. It might feel excruciating right now, but it will pass. All storms eventually do.

The final component of the Equal or Better Principle is growth. You can never go backwards when you are eager to grow and open to learning. Start looking at challenges as learning opportunities—assignments sent to help prepare and better equip you for the challenges yet to come. This is how you bolster your faith, solidify your strength, and embrace any Change: Lean into the chances for growth that present themselves. Regardless of how they show up.

The past has little meaning to me now. But when, on occasion, I look back to ponder it, I do so with the utmost sense of gratitude and appreciation. Everything I endured led me here to this moment writing these words, imparting these truths. Whenever I felt the Universe was telling me no, it was actually saying, *I got you, Chris. Sit back and watch me work my magic.* These days, I have enough awareness and presence to believe it. The road to better is always bumpier than you expect. But damn is it a beautiful ride.

6
Found

STRIPPED OF MEANING

There's a line in *A Course in Miracles* that says, "I must have decided wrongly, because I am not at peace." Peace is only ever one decision, one moment of surrender, one layer of consciousness away. This realization alone can redefine your whole life.

If you want to be at peace, you are the only person, presence, or problem that can stand in the way. Peace is our natural way of being. You aren't born encased in a cloud of conflict, with a heart full of fear, mentally consumed by the second arrow of suffering. You emerge pristine and clean—the physical incarnation of a fresh start. The key to peace, then, is to strip away anything that serves to keep you from this natural state.

Contrary to how it sounds, this is not the avoidance of pain. All of the layers of unconscious stories, coping mechanisms, and resistance techniques you've relied on are what have attempted to do just that: Numb, bury, resist, deny, and avoid your pain. Remember, anything that you resist, persists. Your best judgment is what got you where you are right now, feeling like you've lost your way. In order to find your way back, you must be willing to see things differently and make different choices. You must be willing to experience Change as it arises. You must be willing to surrender your inclination to control. You must be willing to put peace on the pedestal above all else.

You rediscover inner peace by choosing it. You refuse to let anything that happens around you dictate what happens inside of you. You sit through your painful experiences with a higher awareness that the physical sensation will pass and what lies underneath—a reservoir of everlasting love and transcendental calm—will float back to the surface. This isn't about being apathetic about your life. It's actually the opposite. You show the utmost level of care for yourself and others when you do not take on emotional burdens that are not yours to bear. When we make the mistake of doing so, we suffer immensely.

In the end, suffering is the result of searching for meaning in our pain. Attempting to make sense of past pain is in many ways the same as relying on a mirage to guide you through the desert. Pain destabilizes us, makes us scared, drives us mad, and causes us to rely on fear to guide us. We imagine things that are not there. Searching for meaning in the events of our lives is a thirst that can never be quenched. The only meaning an event can possess is the meaning we project upon it in our minds. Thus, our mental thirst is only real if we choose to believe in it. It's important to ask: *Am I really seeing clearly, or am I projecting meaning onto what I perceive?* Inner awareness is crucial to understanding when you're trapped in a deceptive mental mirage of meaning. Searching for meaning keeps us locked in a permanent haze, our ship unable to navigate back to the shore of sanity. Until we notice our automatic negative thoughts, scrutinize our desire to play the victim, and shift our relation to our stories, we carry this baggage with us from the past into the present moment. The thirst remains.

The present is the only moment in time that has any real meaning because it is where life unfolds. When this sinks in, it transforms everything. Your power does not rest in some bygone era in a moment where the tides of Change felt like they would drown you. Your power rests in the proclamation of the present—the reclamation of your holy right to shift your perception and choose again right now. This is how you stop the lies in your mind that keep you rooted in fear and ego and shame. This is how you evolve beyond your scripts. This is how you transcend your traumas. You stop carrying them with you into the present moment. You simply stop assigning meaning to anything other than the now.

This is the crux of any journey: It all unfolds in your mind. Whether you allow it to occur in the dark recesses of the unconscious realm or in the light of mindful consciousness is completely up to you. Whether you stay stuck in the past or embrace the present is completely up to you. Whether you tap into your permanent state of peace or fall into a perpetual state of suffering is completely up to you. Either way, it's an inside job.

Healing, peace, and presence are the noblest goals you can have in this life because they are evidence of the presence of the one thing that is true and right and real. And that is love. The presence of love heals our false perceptions of fear and separation, disillusionment and victimization. Love takes our fearful thoughts and corrects them to right-minded thinking. Strip away everything else and love is all that remains. Instead of searching for meaning, we should look for love—in every interaction, circumstance, and relationship. It is the only thing we truly seek, and the only thing that truly matters. This is how we forgive, how we cultivate gratitude, how we accept grace, how we rebuild our lives, how we keep an open heart, how we experience heartbirth instead of heartbreak, how we excavate peace from within. We make a critical choice to consciously and acutely focus on love and love alone. Everything else is a map to nowhere.

NEVER REALLY LOST

Please read what I am about to say slowly and carefully, taking in each and every word: *The only place you were ever really lost was in your mind.* You did not actually lose yourself. How could you? We've already established that you can't lose something that you are, you can only lose something that you have. You also did not lose your way. There is no one way to live, there is only one now to do it. The single biggest mistake you can make in this life is to get lost in the midst of the unconscious mind instead of trusting the surrendered consciousness within. You do this by over-thinking everything. You only *thought* you lost your way. You only *thought* you wandered from the path meant for you. Instead of allowing yourself to *feel*, you allowed yourself to become consumed in *thought*. Rather than owning the beauty of the moment right in front of you, you made the choice that things aren't right just the way they are. You tried to make sense of the senseless and create order out of Change. Neither of those things are wise because neither are possible.

We trap ourselves mentally when we search for meaning in our painful emotions. This is a turn toward the darkness and away from the light. Please don't spend years digging around in the darkness. Hear me loud and clear when I say that you will freefall into nothing if you do this. Just look for the light and follow it. Become aware enough that you stop yourself from wading around in a pit of mental pain long enough for it to pass. And yes, it will always pass.

The way out of pain is always through feeling it, not trying to interpret it or mull it over in your mind. Whether physical or emotional, learning to sit with the pain of uncertain times, unknown outcomes, and unconscious behavior is one of the hardest tasks you will ever undertake in your life. Do not run away, push down, deny, or avoid these emotional and spiritual learning opportunities. That's how you give birth to suffering in your life.

The way out of suffering is always through stillness and surrender. Give yourself time to slow down. Give up believing in your fear-based stories. Give over your illusion of control. Give into acceptance of anything that cannot be changed. Focus on finding new ways in which you can grow your faith and look for love in whatever circumstances may arise. Everything that shows up in life has something to teach you about the depth of your heart. Let yourself learn instead of running away. Slow down and meditate at the altar of your heart. This is the only requirement to transcend trauma, embrace change, and outlast pain: You choose to see it not as something that will hold you back but as something that will hold you up to light and help you heal. You honor it as you honor any moment—with the reverence, attention, and respect it deserves.

Your mind can be your best friend or it can be your biggest

enemy. It's up to you. If you're feeling lost, perhaps it's time to ask yourself: *Have I really lost my way, or do I just think that's the case?* I can guarantee you it's the latter. You are only ever lost in the fear and darkness of your mind and you are only ever found in the love and light of this very moment. Everything else is an illusion. The sooner you realize this, the sooner you can reclaim what it means to be truly, utterly, imperfectly you. In all your splendor.

In my life, I've realized that the only problem I've faced wasn't any particular situation itself, but rather my *perception* of the situation as a problem to begin with. The unconscious mind will try to trick you into believing that there's always something wrong. I know it did for me. My perception of a situation as a problem was always directly proportional to my lack of faith in the Universe and unwillingness to accept life exactly as it was. My mom's death? *Unacceptable.* My boyfriend cheating on me? *Big problem.* My sister molesting me? *Unconscionable.* Those were not problems per se. They were pieces of information—ephemeral events that transpired. But they did reveal some problems with my perceptions.

Your perceptions can either drag you down in fear or raise you up in love. Once I shifted my perceptions, everything else fell into place accordingly. I realized that I'm not a victim; I just happened to be on the receiving end of behavior caused by somebody's lack of love. And sometimes that lack of love was my own. In the end, it was all a matter of how I chose to see it. That same choice is thankfully, graciously, divinely yours.

Marianne Williamson, spiritual guru and bestselling author of *A Return to Love,* writes: "God is merely the love within us, so returning to Him is a return to ourselves." When you're on the side of love you can never, ever be lost. It's about time we believed that. And made it our first and only priority. No matter what happened in the past or might happen in the future. Look for love and let everything else go. It didn't matter then, and it matters even less now.

FIND YOUR WAY BACK

The walk back is clear. Whatever role we played in feeling lost to begin with, it is always our duty to consciously choose to come home. We return to the path of highest good—to our highest selves—by following a certain set of steps. These steps are the same as the framework for this book, but they are all based on a singular fact: It doesn't matter what happened in the past, your power always rests in your ability to choose differently right now. You take back the throne of your soul by remembering that a higher power ordained you to make right-minded, openhearted, conscientious choices. This, of course, was always the case. You were only ever one choice away from returning home.

The way back is always paved with empathy, kindness, and compassion. Like a mother opening her arms for her baby to return, we are never a sight for sore eyes when we recognize ourselves. Remembering that you are the maker of your choices is a miracle. When you feel trapped in resistance, like everything around you is out of control and falling to pieces, you can choose to face it head-on and not run away. Rather than feel enslaved to the traumatic experiences you endured, you can choose to radically accept them and make peace with the past. As opposed to trying to control all of the variables outside of your reach, you can focus solely on what you have the power to control—even if it means choosing to accept that surrender is your only option.

We complete the homecoming process by remaining openhearted and optimistic whenever a storm threatens to throw us off our perceived course once again. And we embrace the detour that has presented itself as the new direction in which we will progress. This is the essence of the **RACE Model for Change**:

- **Resist** one thing only: Your resistance to Change.
- **Accept** what you can't Change so you may let go.
- **Choose** to Change what you can by reclaiming your power to choose.
- **Embrace** Change by remaining open to it in the future.

Throughout those four key steps, there are many small choices we make that add up to finding our way back to ourselves when we feel lost. We do so by:

- Bringing our shadows to light by becoming aware of unconscious stories, unhealed emotional triggers, and unhealthy behaviors.
- Committing to recognize and relinquish our resistance and release our desire for control.

- Showing up for our life even if it looks different from our expectations, seems difficult at first glance, or feels painful in the moment.
- Learning to allow things to be utterly as they are, without expectation or myopic judgment.
- Allowing ourselves to feel whatever feelings arise, never seeking to protect ourselves from what feels bad or preserve what makes us feel good.
- Radically accepting the past for its certainty and irrevocability through the power of forgiveness, ho'oponopono, gratitude, and grace.
- Focusing on our inner world and outer orbit.
- Choosing people, places, thoughts, feelings, and a life purpose that are encouraging, supportive, and safe for us to express our full selves.
- Embracing change when it shows up in our lives if for no other reason than we know it will help us grow.
- Knowing that the Universe is a friendly place that wants to help you thrive.
- Believing that you are connected to, guided by, and protected by a power of the highest order—and learning to recognize when signs show up.

I don't worry anymore. I know that if I give up resisting, practice radical acceptance, exercise my divine right to choose, and embrace any change—expected or otherwise—that arises from this point forward, I will remain true to my spirit and never feel lost again. And, even if I fail to remember these steps and feel like I've faltered, I'm golden because I'm wrapped in boundless grace in the eyes of my Creator. Who needs worries when you're walking with God?

THE TRIUMPHANT RETURN

The idea of spiritual return is a universal one. It cuts across cultures, transcends time, and traverses space. Nearly every belief system touches on it. Case in point: A minister friend of mine told me about a beautiful tradition in Judaism called Teshuva. Meaning "return" in English, Teshuva is a 10-day period between Rosh Hashanah, the beginning of a new year in the Jewish faith, and Yom Kippur, a day of atonement marked by a strict and solemn fast each year.

Earmarked by the two most important holidays in Judaism, Teshuva is a process of deep reflection and sincere repentance, where Jews take responsibility for their actions and seek atonement for all those times over the past year where they've acted out of alignment with their spirit. It's an annual ritual where Jews ask God for forgiveness for the sins they committed. It is the act of wiping the proverbial moral slate clean. It's an act of turning the page.

The shuv in Teshuva is the Hebrew verb to "turn." Teshuva is a turn inward as we dive headfirst into the wilderness within. It's a turn back to the path of highest good—a course correction in our actions that's based on our reflections. It's a turn back to the light.

Teshuva is an intentional redirection—a resurrection of our morals, our values, and our virtues. It's a chance to shift focus from our ego to our soul. It's an opportunity to drop our gratification and seek God instead. It's a moment to mend our mental wounds with self-compassion.

The return of Teshuva means a return to spirit, a return to the light, a return to love. In doing so, we commit to letting anything else go. We promise to cut through all of our conditioning for the sake of learning, sacrifice our stories for the sake of our soul, and stop making sacrilegious choices that sabotage our best and most holy interests.

The fact that this period of reflection is codified into the Jewish holy calendar is indicative of just how important it is to their faith. What a tremendous sentiment that one can recognize where they've stumbled and can choose again. The encouragement to wash oneself clean and make better choices is extremely emancipating.

This same process of redemption is available to you. You don't need to wait until autumn to return to your true nature. You don't need to wait until a holiday to reflect on your misguided moves. You don't need to wait to make a turn back to the support of a higher power. It is yours if you choose it right now.

Teshuva reminds me of the concept of grace. They are both processes of reconciliation, repentance, and reverence. The unmerited favor of God swoops in to purify those who feel the most damaged, the most damned, and the most destroyed. It's easy to get caught up in life and forget to turn inward and return to love. Teshuva and grace show us that it's not just nice to have; it's necessary to do. In order to rectify our wrongs and cleanse our spirit, we must revisit and reflect on the consequences of our choices. Either way, they are forgiven. But in accepting our atonement we must also make a commitment to make better, healthier, safer, holier, more conscientious choices—to take seriously the gift of life and to honor both the humanness and the holiness of our composition.

In a lot of ways, this brings us full circle on our journey. Throughout this book, we've discussed and reflected on our free will—our God-given right to choose our choices in life. Teshuva marks the close of that cycle, the return back home, the end of one road and the beginning of another. Teshuva isn't just a turn back to what happened before; it's the reminder that with each passing moment we have the chance to make better choices right now. This is a reset. We get to refresh. We are always granted the opportunity to be made new with each and every moment. In that regard, Teshuva is a nod to the fundamental fact that everything remains in flux. Teshuva is a way to honor Change.

Finding your way back to yourself when you feel lost can seem like a bewildering and daunting undertaking. In reality, it's actually quite simple. The way back to the self is really just the way back to God. Since God is love, finding your way simply means searching for, identifying with, and acting upon the love we *are* and the love we *perceive*. It's an acknowledgement of an eternal ache to be one with this force—to transcend our bodies and minds and lean into the indestructible nature of our spirits. This is what Marianne Williamson meant when she wrote, "There is really only one drama going on in life: Our walk away from God, and our walk back. We simply reenact the one drama in different ways."

The *path* of highest good is a reunification with the *force* of highest good. And that force is love. It's the recognition that you are the purest expression of this love—an incarnation of consciousness and an untouchable essence of the Universe. Awakening to this truth inside is what life is all about. Accepting it is our purpose. Returning to it is how we heal. There really is no other way.

> The *path* of highest good is a reunification with the *force* of highest good. And that force is love.

There's a reason why the phrase "home is where the heart is" resonates with so many people. It's because it's true. A return home is just a return to love. Your homecoming will be held in your heart. You must feel it in order to realize it. Any other attempts to find your way are misinformed and misguided. Stop fighting the truth and come home, dear one. Love awaits you.

THE TEN QUESTIONS

There are several questions I've asked myself again and again throughout my healing journey. They're the same questions that I've asked throughout this book. They help to guide me back to right-minded thinking and wholehearted living each and every time they are employed. Whenever I'm feeling triggered, as if I'm slipping from the path of highest good, I return to these questions. They help me ground myself. They help me re-center. They help me focus. They help me to prioritize peace. They help me to feel. They help me to heal. They are mile markers on the journey back to love. I hope they'll do the same for you:

1. **How would I feel if I gave up telling this story?**
   It's rare that we know when we're in a web of lies backed by a story. But asking ourselves this question can help us snap out of our unconsciousness and step back into the peace and reality of the present moment. I often find that identifying a story causes me to justify why I'm employing that story in the first place. Our stories are heavy. Peace is not. Questioning the role our stories play causes us to see through the veil of fear and return more quickly to love. And return to our true selves in the process.

2. **Am I fighting the flow of life?**
   Like the previous prompt, this question helps me recognize when I'm in a state of resistance. Resisting is emotionally draining. Ask yourself: *Is this resistance productive?* This is really a rhetorical question. It's never productive. But framing our resistance in this way helps us see acceptance as the relief we need from the burden we're carrying. Think about this: *What would this situation look like if I just accepted it instead?* Picturing what it would be like to accept a situation as it is helps us see how surrender can be our biggest

saving grace. Just as we're about to exhibit our false sense of control.

3. **When was the last time I let my heart break?**
Change is a fact of life. It is a law of our Universe. Sometimes Change can be painful, like when we don't see it coming or when it doesn't meet our expectations. Allow yourself to feel it. This is the single most important thing we can do when Change feels painful. Pain is a signal from the body or mind. Physical pain is automatic. Emotional pain is as well. But the vast majority of our emotional pain is a result of the web of stories we weave around the memory of an event. Over time, we learn to recoil and retreat from pain. We don't want to feel anything uncomfortable. But the more we avoid our pain, the more of it we perpetuate in our lives. Whenever something painful arises, it is a reminder to feel, not a reminder to think. Ask yourself: *When was the last time I sat with my emotional pain instead of dismissing it or acting on it?* The goal is to feel your pain without shrouding it in stories. This process cannot be rushed. With time and intention, the signal can properly work its way through our system and the energy can be transmuted. The system can recalibrate and return to homeostasis—to peace. We can finally see our heartbreaks as heartbirths.

4. **Will I become what's happened, or will I become what I choose instead?**

    There are many important choices we make as we grow and heal. But one of the most important is whether we will take on the identity of our past or whether we will be made new in the present. Releasing attachment to the past is what allows us to move on. Many folks have a hard time grasping that this is a choice they can make. Their identity is wrapped up in what has happened. They are attached to what it means to them. Once we realize that we are more than what we've endured, we can shed who we thought we were and become who we really are. We can stop clinging to our stories. We can train ourselves not to put fear on the altar of our lives. And finally claim the love available to us right now.

5. **Am I willing to stand in solidarity with myself above all else?**

    The world is caught up in a mass delusion. Many folks live in a perpetual state of fear and suffering. When you commit to healing, you are actively defying this accepted delusion and waking up to a brighter, unaccepted reality. This will be confusing to many people you know who are not as conscious of their fear and suffering—who know no other way than to live in the darkness they've known their entire lives. In order to be successful in healing, you must be willing to do it for you and you alone. Only you can accept this atonement. Shifting your perceptions, your choices, and your life will cause others to judge you. That's okay. Committing to your own path of highest good is all that matters. Everything else is just noise.

6. **What is life asking of me right now?**
   Life is a journey of healing, a return to love, and a conversation with Change. We honor these sacred duties by seeking stillness, being present in the moment, and looking for opportunities to spread the love that we are and the love that we possess. While you were waiting on the Universe to send you a blessing, it was waiting on you to realize that you are the blessing. Once we own this truth, we can fully step into our power. We can choose to be a force for good. We can be the light the world needs. We do this by looking for the opportunities to heal maligned thinking and help spread joy. We do this by asking ourselves: *How can I show up more fully at this moment?* These opportunities are presented to us through shifts and signs. All we have to do is have the courage to look for and accept them. Each and every day.

7. **Do I believe we live in a friendly or hostile universe?**
   Your relationship with life determines your quality of life. We have to decide if we think life is fundamentally for or against us—if we believe the Universe is friendly or hostile. This choice is critical. It informs our outlook, determines our demeanor, and accentuates our

approach to living. Your perception of the world creates your existence within it. I've decided that life is a force of love that unfolds through me and therefore is happening for my benefit. As a part of a larger fabric of consciousness, I recognize that my connection to something greater than me grants me power beyond measure, wisdom beyond the mind, with boundless opportunities to feel and to heal. My reality is shaped by these beliefs. Whenever I fall out of alignment, I ask myself: *Do I believe life is happening to me or for me?* This helps me remember that life, God, and the Universe know better than me. All I need to do is trust and believe. Anything is possible through faith.

8. **Am I really seeing clearly, or am I projecting meaning onto what I perceive?**
The only meaning something can possess is that it shows us where we need to heal, where the key to peace lies, where we need to focus on love. Anything else is a fallacy. The past has died. It is but a memory. The future is yet to be born. How can it hold any meaning if it doesn't exist? The present moment is the only thing that holds any value because it is the only moment at which we experience consciousness. The key to clarity, then, is to step out of the mind-made stories and into the depth of this moment right here and right now. Once we recognize that we're caught in a web of stories about the past or future, we can stop warping the present moment and step more fully into

its power and potential. And bring it into form through our being.

9. **Have I found the love in this situation, or do I need to keep looking?**
If love is all that exists, then it should be all we venture to perceive. There's a seed of love behind every outcry, every action, every emotion. It's our duty to look for it and nurture it. The purpose of this prompt is to reorient us back to love by reminding us to keep looking for it. No matter what.

10. **How can I lose something that I Am?**
You are a conscious being, a bearer of light, and a force of everlasting love made material in this form. Consciousness cannot be destroyed. Light cannot be destroyed. Love cannot be destroyed. They are the very fabric of the Universe and they are the very fabric of who you are. You cannot lose yourself because you cannot lose something that you are. This question is, of course, rhetorical. It is only meant to awaken your awareness within and help you shed your attachment, judgment, and resistance to the truth. You were never lost; you only thought you were. And just because you think something does not make it true.

For me, these questions are a saving grace—guardian angels that escort me back to peace and healing when I veer away from love and into fear. When you feel the familiar sting of suffering, return to this list of questions and reflect. Always remember that peace does not exist in the questions themselves, but rather as a state of being within. These are merely guides. You can add to or remove from this list as you see fit. It is by no means comprehensive. Whatever helps to reorient you back to love and peel away the layers of fearful conditioning. That's all that's important.

THE SEVEN SEMINAL LESSONS

In addition to the questions from the previous chapter, there are seven seminal lessons I've learned on my journey that stand out more than others. They are brilliant bits of truth I've gleaned over the years and across experiences. Together, they form a marvelous mosaic that comforts me when I feel lost, and guides me back to living consciously open instead of unconsciously closed. None of these truths should come as a shock to you. They serve as a recap of the lessons I've imparted throughout this book. Consider them a cheat sheet of sorts for how to find your way back to you when you feel lost. Use them as stepping-stones back to your true compassionate nature when you feel angry or frustrated, anxious or uncertain, listless or sad. Whatever feelings arise, these lessons will always tell you to feel them. I can't guarantee that these lessons will change your life. I can only tell you that they've completely changed mine, and hope that they'll do the same for you.

The first lesson is that **life is a conversation with Change**. Change is the law of life. Our perceptions are made possible through

Change. Our feelings are made possible through Change. Our journey is made possible through Change. So is our growth. Earlier in the book, I wrote that life favors those who converse with Change in a brave, open, and empowering way. Embracing Change is how we have that conversation. Change is a fundamental part of our human experience. The sooner we learn to converse with it, the more effectively we can learn the lessons laid out for us. And the sooner we can step forward on our path of highest good.

The second lesson is: **Pain is automatic, but suffering is a choice**. Life speaks to us in moments big and small, painful and pleasurable, expected and unexpected. These are our assignments. It is our duty to embrace them as they arise and use them as fuel for our enlightenment and evolution. While pain happens automatically and is a natural part of being human, suffering is an unnatural selection we make by refusing to experience Change.

Simply put, suffering is the result of mentally interfering in our experience of Change. This is nothing more than a mental prison we build out of avoidance, denial, and resistance of reality. We create stories to try to make sense of Change. We dig for meaning and try to decipher why it matters. We turn ourselves into victims to get pity and justify our fear of Change. As we discussed, the Buddha called suffering the second arrow. The first arrow is the physical pain we experience. It is often unpredictable and occurs naturally as a result of Change. The second arrow is the mental or emotional pain we experience when things Change. We choose to replay the events over and over in our minds. And we keep reliving the pain as a result.

You do not have to suffer. You can choose acceptance. You can choose healing. You can choose salvation. All you have to do is decide not to interfere with your experience of Change. Feel it. And then let it go. Nothing more and nothing less is required of you. In fact, choosing not to suffer is an active way for you to save your time, energy, and effort. Do less and feel more. That's it.

The next lesson is: **If it's not love, it's a call for it**. Love is all that is real in this life. Looking at our lives through this lens creates a clear distinction. Everything is either love or a request to be loved. Where love is present, goodness and light prevail. Where it is absent, darkness and ego take over. We over-control. We act out in desperation. We fall from grace.

In the end, the way someone treats you is a reflection of how they feel about themselves. If they are kind and honest and compassionate, their cup of love is likely full. If they are rude and misleading and subversive, their cup of love is likely empty. This perspective changes everything. Learn to see your own behavior and the behavior of others through the lens of love. You just might find that there's more love to go around that way.

This next lesson is key: **If you can't change it, change your relationship to it**. The *Serenity Prayer* helps us get clear about our choices. One of the choices we can make is to change our circumstances. This is how we reclaim our power: We wield our ability to choose again. In the event that we can't change our circumstances, we are only left with one choice: Change our relation to them. You can't change death. You can't change the fact that life is constantly changing. You can't change the inevitability of pain. So we must choose to change the way we look at them.

Miracles are just a shift in perception. We move into a miracle mindset when we're willing to see something differently. This is how we revolutionize our lives. We change what we can or we choose to change how we look at what we can't. Nothing else is a productive use of time or energy.

You always have the power to choose differently right now is the fifth seminal lesson. It doesn't matter how many times you messed up. It doesn't matter how many mistakes you made. It doesn't matter what happened in the past. What's done is done. The only meaning that can be derived from the past is the fact that you survived and made it right here to this very moment. Let bygones be bygones. Your ability to make a different choice in the present moment is your ticket out of darkness and back to the light. You can break age-old cycles, rewrite limiting beliefs, and transcend your trauma triggers. Look in the mirror and make a conscious decision that you will make choices that replenish, rejuvenate, and rejoice you. The way back to love is paved with our choices. Never forget that this is your birthright. And always was.

The penultimate lesson is: **Your heart will break sooner or later. Your only job is to let it.** Heartbreak is inevitable. But it's also how we're reborn. Sooner or later, something will occur that will shatter your sense of complacency, defy any and all of your expectations, and feel like it's breaking you apart inside. These are all normal reactions when something unexpected happens. Change is difficult to process. But there is another way. I know this might seem counterintuitive, but when it feels like your heart is breaking—like you're coming apart at the seams—it's not because your life is ending, it's because it's entering a new beginning. You're not experiencing heartbreak; you're experiencing heartbirth. You're not breaking at all; you're being pieced back together. You're just experiencing growing pains. Do not resist, deny, bury, avoid, or numb this experience. When we resist these assignments, we amplify their intensity and cause suffering. You have one job and one job only: When it feels like your heart is shattering, let it. Do not interfere. Give up trying to control the outcome. Just embrace the mélange of messy emotions. It's happening for your ultimate benefit. Those benefits will never be realized unless you allow it to happen. That's all you need to do.

The final seminal lesson of this book is about the purpose of life: **We are meant to live each moment with an open heart.** Sooner or later, something is going to happen that will make you want to shut down, stop trying, and close yourself off. It could be a breakup. It might be a layoff. It may even show up in the form of a global pandemic that completely alters your daily life. Regardless of what it looks like, it will make you not want to feel what you're feeling. It will cause you to resist. Your heart will become closed and your love will be locked inside. This is not meant to sound alarmist. It is actually a blessing in disguise. Recognizing your inclination to close is the beginning of ensuring that you remain open. Anything is possible with an open heart. Change can't shake you in this state. Pain won't break you in this state. Wholehearted living is a foundation of faith. When you remain open, you send a signal to the Universe that you trust and believe that it will deliver you to something Equal or Better than what you're currently going through. An open heart paves the way when you feel lost because it's how we rediscover presence, love, and God. There is nothing greater or more rewarding than this return. And it starts by choosing not to close.

Brick by brick, these crucial truths lay out important steps to take along your path of highest good. While they are helpful reminders, they are not in and of themselves the end goal. Like the questions from the previous chapter, they can help you find what you seek by assisting you in unlocking and uncovering it from within. They are reserved for those brave and valiant spiritual warriors on a quest for truth. If you've made it this far in your journey, I think it's safe to say that applies to you. So, go forth and wield them. Then pass them on. This world always needs more healers, more unconditional lovers, and more light bearers. You are ordained to help the world awaken. And you do so by awakening yourself. Over and over.

IT'S GOOD TO SEE ME AGAIN

The sky is strewn with cotton candy fire tonight. Cherry blossom petals dance through the air beckoned by a soft breeze. Boisterous birds chirp in the crowded chorus of nearby trees. Another day comes to a close, another page turns in the story of life, another cycle nears its end. A changing of the guards is occurring right on time. I am reminded once more of the impermanence of all things, of the omnipresence of Change. As the light fades, a rich shade of dark indigo settles above the remaining wisps of gold and fuchsia on the horizon—an ocean of air tempering the fiery hues until they are extinguished with the fading daylight. At this moment, everything is harmonious. It feels *right*.

I catch a glimpse of myself in the windowpane and marvel at the man I've become. I see beyond form—beyond my eyes, past my physical features, to the other side of my fragile exterior—and into a realm of indestructible and infinite wisdom within. I know that nothing that happened in the past has power over me in the present. I know that what once hurt me brought me here. I know that I am safe and protected by a power greater and more compassionate than my wildest imagination. I am overcome with gratitude.

I'm grateful to have learned my lessons. I'm grateful that I released my resentments. I'm grateful that I accepted my anguish. I'm grateful that I survived. I'm grateful that I've realized I am a presence of love. These reflections humble me and remind me of how far I've come—and how far I have left to go.

I've spent most of my life running away. Desperate to avoid discomfort, I sought out whatever would restore a sense of ease, false or otherwise. I suppressed my power to consciously choose. I substituted sex and alcohol for the experience of Change. I subverted my best interests. Whatever it took to justify not feeling the bad stuff and only feeling the good.

As a teenager I would've told you that I was in the driver's seat of my life, fully in control of all possible variables and cognizant of all potential variations or deviances from my plan. Once, when I was around 15 years old, I packed a bag and walked three miles to my best friend's house. In a pair of sneakers. In the middle of the worst blizzard in Baltimore's history at the time. I ventured out on my own, braving the harsh conditions just so I wouldn't have to spend what I felt would be a boring few days stuck at home with my dad. 18 months later, he had a debilitating stroke and nearly died.

Reflecting back on this choice in light of my father's condition, I felt guilty. I never considered how that must've made him feel. I never imagined he'd be incapacitated and holding on by a thread. In that hospital room, I sensed the seeds of something life-changing. It took many years to grow within me, but the realization was planted deep within. The only person I was running away from was *me*.

These days, my father and I reminisce about that blizzard and laugh at my incorrigibility. We've let any attachments to the weight of that moment go. We appreciate and love one another. We know better now. Growth.

I return to my reflection in the window and smile. I see my dad in the wrinkles that have formed around my eyes. I see my mom in the dimples that have formed in my cheeks. I see my sister in the button at the end of my nose. At this moment, I am connected to them. I see how they've each shaped the mound of clay I used to be and molded me into the imperfect man I am, standing here in reverie. I recognize how beautifully their lives have influenced mine. I see the web of choices that got us all here. And I see how differently things could've played out. My mother and sister both could've lived. They could've made better choices. They had endless chances at a fresh start and they let them slip away.

I am reminded of how precious time is, how feeble our bodies are, how meaningless everything becomes in the great equalizer of death. It is yet another reminder to live while you can, to focus only on the now, and to do so with purpose, clarity, and intention. At least that's what I intend to do. If you also choose to live your life in this way, please know that being lost is really a misnomer. Losing yourself just means you've forgotten yourself; finding yourself means remembering who you are.

I have one final acronym to share with you. It will help you focus as you find your way forward and remember who you are. I call it the **Spiritual ACL**. It stands for **Always Choose Light**. The light symbolizes your goodness, your holiness, your love, your consciousness, your understanding, your compassion, and your truth. When life feels heavy, like the weight of the world is pushing down upon you, do not run away or suppress how you feel. Whenever things feel dark and dreary, you choose light by defying the pull of darkness in your unconscious mind. Do not act on it. It will eventually subside. Choosing light means choosing to remember that Change is the one constant, that all things are temporary.

When the sting of trauma untold starts to tug at your heartstrings, threatening to pull you into a fear story or a shame spiral once again, become aware instead. Notice how your energy shifts. Realize that you can choose not to indulge these protective impulses as they arise within you. You can remind yourself that you are safe no matter what. You can rewrite the darkness of the past with the decision you make right now to choose this awareness, this light. When you slip into resistance and you want things to be different than they are, allow the light to slip in next to it and you'll see that things are in perfect order as they are. When you feel stuck, like you've reached the end of the road and there are no more choices you can possibly make, reach for the light. It'll bring you to the mirror of your soul and help you see yourself clearly. It will show you that there's always another choice. You are never trapped. How could you be? *You are the light.*

This has been a voyage of hope, a journey of resilience, and a conversation with Change. My biggest wish is that this book inspires you to have your own return to love, your own reconciliation with life, your own conversation with Change. And that you show up no matter what. Do this and you will reap the fruits of a life well lived. Do this and you will never truly be lost. Do this and you will finally realize *it's good to see me again.*

You are never trapped. How could you be?
You are the light.

Printed in Great Britain
by Amazon